CANCEL CULTURE

Also by Alan Dershowitz

CANCEL CULTURE

The Latest Attack on
FREE SPEECH
and
DUE PROCESS

ALAN DERSHOWITZ

HOT BOOKS

This book is dedicated to the students who are standing up, often at personal risk, to cancel culture, political correctness, identity politics, and other attacks on free speech, due process, meritocracy, and democratic values.

Hot Books may be purchased in bulk at special discounts for sales promotion, corporate gifts, fund-raising, or educational purposes. Special editions can also be created to specifications. For details, contact the Special Sales Department, Skyhorse Publishing, 307 West 36th Street, 11th Floor, New York, NY 10018 or info@skyhorsepublishing.com.

Hot Books® and Skyhorse Publishing® are registered trademarks of Skyhorse Publishing, Inc.®, a Delaware corporation.

Visit our website at www.hotbookspress.com.

10 9 8 7 6 5 4 3 2

Library of Congress Cataloging-in-Publication Data is available on file.

Print ISBN: 978-1-5107-6490-3
eBook: 978-1-5107-6491-0

Cover design by Brian Peterson

Printed in the United States of America

Table of Contents

CANCEL CULTURE

Introduction

Cancel culture is the new McCarthyism of the "woke" generation. As with the old McCarthyism, it ends careers, destroys legacies, breaks up families, and even causes suicides—with no semblance of due process or opportunity to disprove the often-false or exaggerated accusations. As with McCarthyism, even when the accusations are true, or partially true, they are generally about acts done, statements made, or positions taken many years earlier, when different values and attitudes prevailed. And, as with McCarthyism, the impact goes beyond the cancelled individual and affects other members of society, from audiences denied the right to hear cancelled performers, to students denied the right to learn from cancelled teachers, to citizens denied the right to vote for cancelled politicians.

I remember the original McCarthyism and the devastating impact it had on my generation of young people. We were warned by our parents never to speak out, sign petitions, join organizations, or attend concerts that were in any way associated with left-wingers, "pinkos," or fellow travelers, lest we be labeled "subversive" and our future prospects cancelled. My parents, especially my mother, were terrified about "lists" and "records." This was, after all, the age of "blacklists," "Red Channels," and other colored compilations that kept anyone on them from getting a job. "They will put you on a list," my mother would warn. Or, "It will go on your permanent record." When I was fourteen, I actually did something that may have gotten me on a list.

It was during the height of the McCarthy period, shortly after Julius and Ethel Rosenberg had been sentenced to death for allegedly spying for the Soviet Union. A Rosenberg relative was asking people to sign a petition to save the Rosenbergs' lives. I read the petition and it made sense to me, so I signed it. A neighbor observed the transaction and duly reported it to my mother. She was convinced that my life was over, my career ruined, and my willingness to sign a Communist-inspired petition part of my permanent record. My mother decided that I had to be taught a lesson. She told my father the story. I could see that my father was proud of what I had done, but my mother told him to slap me. Ever obedient, he did, causing him, I suspect, more pain than me.

During the height of McCarthyism, we couldn't see movies, go to shows, or watch TV programs made by or acted in by blacklisted artists,[1] because there were none. We couldn't be taught by blacklisted teachers, because they were fired. We couldn't be patients, clients, or voters for blacklisted doctors, lawyers, or politicians, because they were denied the ability to practice their professions.

Even more fundamentally, the old McCarthyism endangered our constitutional rights of free speech and due process, which are the core protectors of liberty and barriers against tyranny. The new McCarthyism—cancel culture—threatens these rights as well.

One dictionary recently selected "cancel culture" as "the word of the year" because "it has become, for better or worse, a powerful force."[2] The most famous United States dictionary, Merriam-Webster, has posted a lengthy description in its section "Words We're Watching," which are "words we are increasingly seeing in use but that have not yet met our criteria for entry." According to

---

1   Some blacklisted artists engaged in subterfuges to work. See *The Front* for a fictional film version of this phenomenon.

2   *Australian Macquarie Dictionary*, December 2019. The Committee's Choice & People's Choice word of the Year 2019, December 9, 2019, available at https://www.macquariedictionary.com.au/resources/view/word/of/the/year.

Merriam-Webster, "Cancel is getting a new use." Whereas in previous usages, cancelling referred to cancelling an object, such an event or a subscription, now "canceling and cancel culture has to do with the removing of support for public figures in response to their objectionable behavior or opinions. This can include boycotts or refusal to promote their work. [I]n the latest use of the word, you can cancel people—in particular, celebrities, politicians, or anyone who takes up space in the public consciousness. To cancel someone (usually a celebrity or other well-known figure) means to stop giving support to that person. The act of canceling could entail boycotting an actor's movies or no longer reading or promoting a writer's words. The reason for a cancellation can vary, but it usually is due to the person in question having expressed an objectionable opinion, or having conducted themselves in a way that is unacceptable, so that continuing to patronize that person's work leaves a bitter taste." Merriam-Webster then goes on to explain the origin of the term:

> "The idea of canceling—and as some have labeled it, cancel culture—has taken hold in recent years due to conversations prompted by #MeToo and other movements that demands greater accountability from public figures. The term has been credited to Black users of Twitter, where it has been used as a hashtag. As troubling information came to light regarding celebrities who were once popular such as Bill Cosby, Michael Jackson, Roseanne Barr, and Louis C.K.—so come calls to cancel such figures. The cancellation is akin to a cancelled contract, a severing of the relationship that once linked a performer to their fans.[3]"

There are some who still argue, in the face of overwhelming evidence to the contrary, that the entire phenomenon of cancel culture is an exaggeration concocted by the right to discredit the left.[4] I

---

3   *Merriam Webster*, available at https://www.merriam–webster.com/words-at-play/cancel-culture-words-were-watching.

4   See Osita Nwanevu, *The Cancel Culture Con*, New Republic, Sept. 23, 2019.

leave it to the readers, after reviewing the evidence in this book, to decide for themselves.

A. The Illegitimate Ancestors of Cancel Culture

Cancel culture, though a child of the current woke generation, is an illegitimate descendant of both hard-right McCarthyism and hard-left Stalinism.

The difference, of course, is that both McCarthyism and Stalinism employed the power of government, whereas cancel culture employs the power of public opinion, social media, threats of economic boycotts, and other constitutionally protected forms of private action. This power is magnified by the pervasiveness and speed of the internet and social media, which are the weapons of choice deployed by cancel culture. Winston Churchill reportedly quipped that "A lie travels around the globe while the truth is putting on its shoes." That was before the internet. Today, the truth can't even find its shoes.

McCarthyism's most potent weapon was not the subpoena or the contempt power of Congress—though they were indeed powerful weapons of oppression. Its most powerful and pervasive impact was on private individuals, corporations, educational institutions, and the media of the day. Once a person was labelled as a Communist, fellow traveler, red, pinko, or any other term associated with Communism, that person was cancelled. He or she could no longer participate in public life in America. They were cancelled.

There is a story, perhaps apocryphal, that represents the pervasiveness and promiscuousness of this guilt by association. City College, in Manhattan, was a hotbed of radicalism and political activism. One day there was a Communist demonstration, and the police came in to break it up. A policeman hit one demonstrator on the head. The demonstrator shouted out, "Don't hit me. I am an anti-communist." The policeman said, "I don't care what kind of a communist you are," and continued to beat him. Any association with the word communist was enough to cancel, erase, destroy, defame, and marginalize the person associated with that term.

The same is true with today's cancel culture. A mere accusation of racism, sexism, homophobia, anti-Muslim bias, or failure to support Black Lives Matter or the #MeToo movement is enough to get an innocent person cancelled, especially if he is not within the new privileged groups in the "identity politics" of the woke generation.

Some of the ammunition for cancel culture is provided by the #MeToo movement, which does much good in exposing real predators, but often fails to distinguish the guilty from the innocent, or to calibrate degrees of guilt, because it provides no process for disproving false or overstated accusations.

In the vast majority of cancellations, the accusation is a matter of degree, and the question is whether cancellation is proportionate to sins committed. The cancelled person is accused of sexual misbehavior and admits that he had a relationship with his accuser, but claims it was consensual. Or, he admits that he went over the line, but argues that it was a three, rather than an eight, on a scale of ten. In some cases, the cancelled person admits everything, but argues that the good he previously did should be taken into account and that total cancellation is too severe a remedy.

In a few cases—the false accusation against me being the prime example—there are no matters of degree. The alleged offense either occurred or didn't occur. Somebody deserves to be cancelled, but the question is, should it be the accused or the accuser?

In my case, there is no gray area. My accuser has sworn that she had sex with me on six or seven occasions in locations where my travel records prove I could not possibly have been. Her own lawyer has admitted, in a recorded conversation, that after reviewing my travel records, he was convinced that it would have been impossible for me to have been in those locations during the relevant time period and that she was "wrong . . . simply wrong" to accuse me. I have sworn under oath, subject to pains of perjury, that I never met my accuser, never had sex with an underage person, never had sex with anyone related to Jeffrey Epstein, and had sexual contact with only one woman during the relevant time period, namely, my wife of thirty-four years. Notwithstanding this overwhelming evidence of my total innocence, I have been cancelled by some venues and media because, once accused, there is no presumption of innocence. Even worse, there is an irrebuttable presumption of guilt that cannot be rebutted by mere factual evidence, regardless of how convincing and conclusive it may be. The accusation *is* the conviction. Hence, the title of my recent book: *Guild by Accusation: The Challenge of Proving Innocence in the Age of #MeToo*. In the brave new world of cancel culture, there is no room for due process, or any process.

What makes cancel culture even more dangerous in some ways than McCarthyism and Stalinism is that when the government cancels, the victim at least knows who is doing the cancelling. In America, there may be recourse to the courts, and indeed, some courts did do justice to false victims of McCarthyism. But in the current cancel culture, the cancellers are often invisible, anonymous, not accountable. The social media is judge and jury. Accusations over the internet take on a life of their own through Twitter, Facebook, and other largely unregulated platforms on which false accusers have the freedom to defame, destroy, and cancel. Nobody knows their agenda, their biases, their corruptibility. Cancel culture is Kafkaesque in the sense that Joseph K had no idea who his tormentor was, why he was being tormented, or what he had done to warrant his uncertain fate.

Stalinism was, of course, different, in that the power of the state was unlimited and pervasive. Stalin had the power not only to cancel, but to kill.

In 1974, I traveled to the Soviet Union to represent political dissidents and Jewish refuseniks. While there, I encountered Soviet-style cancel culture with my own eyes. I traveled with former General and Professor Telford Taylor, who had been America's chief prosecutor at the Nuremberg trials. We went to a museum of those pathbreaking trials because Professor Taylor wanted to see how they were portrayed nearly thirty years later. He was shocked to look at photographs in which several of the Soviet participants had simply been erased.[5]

We made inquiries and discovered that Stalin always ordered the erasure from photographs of people whom he had cancelled from Soviet history. Some of these people had been arrested, tried, and executed for anti-Soviet activities. Others had simply been erased for expressing "politically incorrect" views. Recall that the very term political correctness was coined during the Stalin regime to impose limits on free speech, free thought, and other liberties. Anyone who deviated from the communist party's line of political correctness risked his or her freedom, legacy, and life.

Those responsible for doctoring the photographs of the Nuremberg trials had done a good job covering up the cancellations. They had photo-shopped the pictures in a seamless manner so that nobody who was not familiar with the original could tell the difference. General Taylor was in several of the pictures, so he could easily see who had been cancelled. He pointed to spaces and said that's where so-and-so stood in the picture. It was Stalin's way of demonstrating who was in charge of making history and what happened to people who tried to exercise basic freedoms, including free-speech, dissent, and other democratic rights.

There are many similarities between the zealots of the current woke generation and the Stalinists of the 1930s and McCarthyites of the 1950s. None of these ideologies brook dissent. They know what's right and what's wrong. They can distinguish the Truth from the Big Lie without the need for debate. They are purists and they sit in judgment over the impure. As Andrew Sullivan has put it in the context of the Black Lives Matter movement after the killing of George Floyd:

> The new orthodoxy . . . seems to be rooted in what journalist Wesley
> Lowery calls "moral clarity." [J]ournalism needs to be rebuilt around

---

5   In Jewish tradition, we curse our enemies with the phrase "yimach shumo," which literally means "his name should be erased from memory." Stalin made a policy of erasing his enemies from history by taking their faces out of photographs.

the moral clarity, which means ending its attempt to see all sides
of a story when there is only one, and dropping even an attempt at
objectivity (however unattainable that ideal might be). And what
is the foundational belief of such moral clarity? That America is
systemically racist, and a white-supremacist project from the start,
that, as Lowery put it . . . "the justice system—in fact, the entire
American experiment—was from its inception designed to perpet-
uate racial inequality."

The concept of "moral clarity" is similar to what I have called in my
book *The Case for Liberalism in an Age of Extremism* "The Truth"—
the idea that there is only one correct way to see things, and that
anyone who disagrees with these views is racist, morally inferior, or
politically incorrect.

The cancel culture eschews the need for due process, or any
process for reaching the truth through evidence and justice. Its
advocates are impatient. They want what they want and they
want it now! Free speech and due process be damned as unnecessary barriers to their utopia. But the denial of free speech and due
process is the sure throughway to dystopia and the tyranny of the
right or left.

B. The Impact of Cancel Culture on Free Speech and Due Process

Two of the most important hallmarks of liberty and democracy are
contained in the American Bill of Rights: "the freedom of speech"
and the "due process of law." These fundamental rights are also
the processes of choice through which free societies conduct the
never-ending search for the truths on which policies should be
based.

These safeguards serve as roadblocks against tyranny. No government in history has achieved liberty for its citizens while denying
them the twin rights of free speech and due process. These fundamental rights are twins in the sense that both reflect skepticism that

governments (or other powerful institutions) have a monopoly over truth. They also represent a trust in the people to evaluate competing truths through processes such as the open marketplace of ideas and the presentation of evidence.

Neither freedom of speech nor due process of law are guarantors of liberty, democracy, or truth, since they both rely on the intelligence and goodwill of fallible human beings. As the great Judge Learned Hand wisely observed:

> "Liberty lies in the hearts of men and women; when it dies there, no constitution, no law, no court can save it; no constitution, no law, no court can even do much to help it. The spirit of liberty is the spirit which is not too sure that it is right; the spirit of liberty is the spirit which seeks to understand the minds of other men and women; the spirit of liberty is the spirit which weighs their interests alongside its own without bias."

The best example of Hand's caveat about liberty living and dying in the hearts of men and women was the election of Hitler in the Weimar Germany of 1932—a nation that before the advent of Nazism boasted of a high level of legal protection for freedom of speech and due process. German voters—at least a plurality of them—were prepared to support the prospect of tyranny in exchange for the promise of economic and other benefits. When liberty died in their hearts, the law could not resurrect or rescue it.

There are few, if any, examples of the opposite phenomenon: liberty without freedom of speech and due process. This is partly tautological, since liberty *includes* freedom of speech and due process. But liberty also transcends these two basic rights. It includes freedom of action, freedom to own and use property, freedom to practice one's religion, freedom to educate one's children, freedom to have an abortion, freedom to engage in homosexual conduct and to make other physical and emotional choices—and, for some, freedom to own guns. It also includes, in the words of Justice Brandeis, "the right to be left alone" by the state, unless there are compelling reasons for intrusion.[6] Without the right to advocate these and other freedoms and to demand due process before they are taken way, our liberty would be in grave danger.

So, in the end, freedom of speech and due process are necessary, even if insufficient, preconditions for and components of liberty, democracy, and truth. They are also generally matters of degree. No society, even the most democratic, has ever allowed total and unrestricted freedom of speech. There are always some limits. Nor has any society, even the least democratic, ever succeeded in totally restricting this freedom. Dissidents almost always manage to communicate by Samizdat[7] or other surreptitious means. Most repressive governments also have some process for evaluating evidence, but it is often so result-oriented and peremptory as to be no real process, and certainly not due process. The same is true today of some university "processes" for determining guilt, especially in the context of sexual accusations.[8]

Justice Felix Frankfurter reminded us that the "the history of liberty has largely been the history of observance of procedural safeguards"—meaning the due process of law. When due process dies, liberty dies along with it.

Though all rights are inevitably matters of degree, it is not difficult to distinguish among governments that are essentially democratic and those that are essentially repressive. Canada does not extend its freedom of speech to certain types of "hate" advocacy. I personally disagree with that limitation, but I would never suggest that Canada is anything but an open, free democracy whose citizens have basic liberties. China, on the other hand, may have some limited freedom of speech and some due process, but few would deny

---

6   See Chapter 9 dealing with vaccines.

7   Samizdat is the Russian word for self-published, usually referring to dissident literature circulated from hand to hand. When I went to the Soviet Union in the 1970s, I saw Samizdat copies of Leon Uris's book *Exodus* being passed around.

8   For example, Harvard's sexual harassment policy is so one-sided that it lacks basic due process rights to the accused party. I, along with twenty-seven colleagues at the law school, have criticized the university for this policy in an open letter in the *Boston Globe*. See Matthew Q. Clarida, "Law School Profs Condemn New Sexual Harassment Policy" *The Harvard Crimson*, Oct. 15, 2014. Efforts are now underway to improve this.

that it is essentially repressive. In the middle, there are countries such as Singapore, which severely restricts—but doesn't eliminate—both freedom of speech and due process for dissents, but its average citizens live decent lives with some degree of liberty.

All this is by way of introduction to the main thesis of this short book: namely, that the new cancel culture in the United States (and other Western democracies) poses a great danger to at least two of our most cherished and important rights: freedom of speech and due process. Even more significantly, this danger comes not from evil tyrants, but rather from people who consider themselves "woke," "do-gooders," and "progressives." Many are motivated by good values and a desire to make our world better and fairer. But, as Justice Louis Brandeis warned: "The greatest dangers to liberty lurk in insidious encroachment by men [and women] of zeal, well-meaning but without understanding."

Many of the current zealots are young students and faculty—men and women alike—who may well become our future leaders. For the first time in my lifetime, academic "justifications" have been offered by hard-left American professors for restrictions on free speech and due process, labeling these fundamental rights as weapons of "privilege," deployed against the unprivileged. (In Europe, there were Fascist and Communist professors who made these arguments in defense of Hitler and Stalin, but not in America until now.)[9] And many radical students are buying into these anti-liberal arguments in the name of cancelling those who they believe are abusing privilege.

So this danger to liberty may reflect a continuing trend rather than merely a temporary phase. If this trend becomes the new reality, it will result in the death, or at least the wounding, of freedom of speech and due process. Hence this requiem for the demise of liberty, which I hope is premature, but which I fear may come about unless we work hard to reverse the current trend—unless we cancel cancel culture.

---

9   But see discussion of Professor Herbert Marcuse in Chapter 1.

C. Cancel culture context and creativity

One of the great dangers of cancel culture is that it stifles creativity. Intellectuals are terrified about being cancelled if speculations made years earlier are wrenched out of context and become weaponized in the war against political incorrectness. My friend and teaching colleague, Steven Pinker, is a perfect example of this dangerous phenomenon.

When Steve and I taught together, he was well known for his creativity, ingenuity, and willingness to explore controversial ideas. Indeed, one of the courses we taught together was entitled "Taboo." It focused on issues that cannot be discussed and debated in today's universities. I don't know whether recordings were made of our classes, but I do know that we threw out ideas in order to encourage students to think, challenge, and come to their own conclusions. It would be easy for a current canceller to wrench out of context some statements each of us made in the course of this didactic exercise. The students back then loved the course, especially its focus on taboo ideas. But today's cancellers might very well assume that every idea that was thrown out for discussion represented our carefully though-through, definitive opinions on controversial subjects. That would be a serious mistake, as the cancellers well know, but ignore in the interest of deploying their weapon against those of whom they disapprove.

Pinker and I were both tenured professors who did not fear university reprisals for expressing controversial views. Indeed, one of the people we invited to the class was the president of Harvard, whom we both criticized openly. In retrospect, it seems that the treatment accorded President Lawrence Summers was one of the opening salvos in the cancellation campaign. He was forced to resign—an early form of cancellation—for speculating out loud about some of the reasons why women have not achieved the same level of success in STEM as men. Whether he was right or wrong about what he said should make no difference in a university setting. If he was wrong, his ideas should be refuted in the open marketplace. Instead, he was cancelled as president of Harvard. A cartoon in a local paper illustrated the double standard applied to cancellation even back then.

It portrayed Summers pleading for his job and saying: "I didn't mean that women are intellectually inferior. I meant that Israel is an apartheid country. Now can I have my job back?"

The Boston Globe quoted me as comparing the tribulation of Summers to the "Trial of Galileo":

> In my 41 years at Harvard, I have never experienced a president more open to debate, disagreement, and dialogue than Larry Summers," wrote Dershowitz, adding that "professors who are afraid to challenge him are guilty of cowardice."
>
> Dershowitz noted that he disagreed with Summers's comments last month that innate differences might help explain why more men than women are top achievers in science and math, but he defended the university president's right to raise the proposition.
>
> "This is truly a time of crisis for Harvard," he wrote. "The crisis is over whether a politically correct straightjacket will be placed over the thinking of everybody in this institution by one segment of the faculty."[10]

Among Summers's other defenders was Professor Pinker, who argued that the empirical issue raised by Summers should be "determined by research, not Fatua."

The firing of Summers was an early manifestation of what has become cancel culture, but the situation has gotten worse over the past fifteen years.

Young professors and students trying to survive today's cancel culture will be deterred and disincentivized from saying anything that might come back to haunt or cancel them in years to come. Cancel culture has no statute of limitations. It goes back to the earliest days of a person's career.

There are those who are now trying to cancel Professor Pinker for views he has expressed over his long and distinguished career. I tend to agree with many of his views, but even if I did not, I would

10 Marcella Bombardieri, "Some Professors back Harvard's Summers", *Boston Globe*, February 17, 2005.

defend his right to be controversial and to ask difficult questions whose truthful answers may be politically incorrect.

The attempt to cancel or at least deplatform him reflects another disturbing consequence of the cancel culture: its negative effect on centrist liberals is greater than on right-wing conservatives. This disparity results from the reality that right-wing conservatives have their own large constituency, which will continue to invite them to present their views, regardless of cancel culture. These include conservative universities, such as Liberty University, as well as conservative think tanks, talk radio, podcasts, and TV stations. But there are few, if any, comparable outlets for centrist liberals who have been cancelled, especially since cancel culture has its greatest impact on campuses and liberal venues.

Even leftists are sometimes cancelled by those to the left of them, as illustrated by a recent story in *The New York Times*. Professor Adolph Reed, who is a Black Marxist scholar at the University of Pennsylvania, was invited to speak to the Democratic Socialists of America's New York City chapter. Professor Reed planned on arguing that the left's focus on the disproportionate impact of COVID-19 on Blacks undermined multiracial organizing. Throughout his distinguished career, Professor Reed has argued that race is an overstated concept and that the focus should rather be on class in a deeply unjust society. This position was offensive for some. They argued that Professor Reed's downplaying of racism was "cowardly and cedes power to the racial capitalists." So the Democratic Socialists of America cancelled his talk.[11]

A crowning irony of cancel culture was when 150 public intellectuals, professors, and writers wrote a letter protesting cancel culture[12] and did not include me among the signatories, despite my long history of defending freedom of speech, my extensive publications, and my fifty years as a professor. The only reason I was not asked to sign—while others far-less accomplished and well-known were

---

11 Michael Powell, "A Black Marxist Scholar Wanted to Talk About Race. It Ignited a Fury", *The New York Times*, August 14, 2020.

12 "A Letter on Justice and Open Debate," Harper's Magazine (October 2020 issue), available at https://harpers.org/a-letter-on-justice-and-open-debate/.

asked—is that I have been cancelled even by those who organized the letter opposing cancel culture. Nevertheless, the substance of the letter reflects my views, and I am including it as an appendix.

D. Cancellation in Politics

Cancel culture has infected politics as well. Viable candidates have been cancelled and precluded from running for higher office because they did not act politically correctly when they were prosecutors or defense attorneys. Among the leading candidates to be nominated by Joe Biden for Vice President was Senator Amy Klobuchar. But then it was alleged that, as a prosecutor, she failed to prosecute policemen who allegedly violated the rights of African-American citizens. This doomed her candidacy and led her to withdraw from consideration. Even Kamala Harris, who was eventually selected, was opposed by many in cancel culture because as a prosecutor she did not go after policemen with sufficient aggressiveness.

These and other similar cancellations and near-cancellations will have a deleterious impact on the criminal justice system. It will incentivize prosecutors always to indict for the highest possible crimes and not use their judgment and discretion in an appropriate manner. Former United States Attorney Alex Acosta was forced to resign as Secretary of Labor because he made a deal with Jeffrey Epstein, whom I represented, that was criticized by members of the public. The impact on prosecutorial discretion from these cancellations is impossible to gauge, but clearly, it will incentivize prosecutors always to overcharge. What has come to be known as the "Acosta effect" will lead prosecutors who don't want to experience what Acosta experienced to err on the side of overcharging. This will have a devastatingly negative impact on the fairness of our judicial system.

Cancel culture also has an impact on electoral politics. Senator Al Franken was forced to resign as the result of accusations that did not rise to the level of criminal or even civil wrongs. Joe Biden was threatened with cancellation on the basis of highly questionable

allegations. But President Trump survived even more serious accusations because his base is far less supportive of cancel culture and
#MeToo than Democrats and liberals. Supreme Court Justices Brett
Kavanaugh and Clarence Thomas survived cancellation because
they, too, had the support of conservatives.

E. Cancel Culture's Impact on Business and the Economy

Among the subjects of cancel culture are business leaders from all
aspects of the economy. Those fired or forced to resign have included
the CEO of McDonald's, the chairman of Amazon Studios, the
Senior Vice President of News at NPR, the head of Fox News, the
Chief Executive of Barnes and Noble, the CEO of CBS, and two
executives at the Humane Society. These were just a few among
many whose business careers were cancelled, some for just cause,
others for questionable allegations.

Private businesses, of course, are entitled to dismiss any employees—from the CEO to workers—based on allegations of misconduct.
The problem is that under cancel culture, businesses may be forced
by public opinion and economic pressure to cancel people who may
very well be innocent of the charges. Often, they are cancelled as
soon as the charges are made, without any opportunity to rebut them
or provide contrary evidence. Sometimes the accusations are true.
Sometimes they are false. Often, they are matters of degree, and it
is difficult to determine whether the degree of culpability warrants
total cancellation.

F. Cancel Culture and the Media

An example of how a false and defamatory media report can result in
the cancellation of a good person who has done excellent work over
a lifetime is what happened to Linda Fairstein, a former prosecutor
and best-selling author. Fairstein was the chief prosecutor in the

Central Park Five case, which may well have resulted in an injustice and erroneous convictions. Reasonable people could disagree about whether she was in any way responsible for the miscarriage of justice, but Netflix simply made up a "series of facts" which were totally untrue. They portrayed her as having led the initial investigation at the scene of the crime and making decisions that impacted the rest of the case. The truth is that Fairstein had not even been assigned to the case at that time. But, because it was shown on Netflix, it was believed to be true by large numbers of people, and Fairstein was cancelled.[13] She was forced to resign as a trustee of Vassar College, and book contracts, appearances, and awards were rescinded. She became a pariah among the woke and progressive cancellers. She is now suing Netflix for defamation, as am I.

I am suing because Netflix broke its promise to me that if I gave them all the documentation proving that I never met my false accuser, they would present this evidence on the air. I was interviewed by Netflix and I laid out the evidence in detail. I also provided them with tapes, emails, and other indisputable documentation, all of which they deep-sixed and never put on the air. Instead, they presented my false accuser as a credible woman with no evidence of lack of credibility. It was this mendacious Netflix series, called *Filthy Rich*, that resulting in my cancellation or deplatforming among many in cancel culture.

Another example is the cancellation of Woody Allen. I was one of Mia Farrow's lawyers in her lawsuit against Allen. I don't know, of course, whether Allen did anything illegal or improper with Mia's daughter, Dylan. But the matter was thoroughly investigated back when the accusation of wrongdoing was made. The Yale-New Haven Hospital investigated and found that "It is our expert opinion that Dylan was not sexually abused by Mr. Allen. Further, we believe that Dylan's statements on videotape and her statements to

---

13 See, e.g., Noah Goldberg, "Central Park Five Prosecutor Resigns from Vassar Board After Student Outcry", *Brooklyn Eagle*, June 4, 2018. The article also mentions that "In 2018, Fairstein—now a writer of mystery novels—won an award from the Mystery Writers of America. After backlash about her role in the Central Park Five Case, the organization decided to rescind the award."

us during our evaluation do not refer to actual events that occurred to her on August 4th, 1992."[14] The matter receded from public view for many years and Allen continued to make his films. Then came the #MeToo movement and cancel culture. With no new evidence, Allen was cancelled. His book and film contracts were violated. He, too became a pariah, though the evidence suggests he may have done nothing wrong. The accusation became the conviction and cancel culture kicked in.[15]

G. The Pervasive Power of Cancel Culture

The power of cancel culture to influence history was brought home to me personally and dramatically when I received a phone call from an obituary writer for the *Washington Post*. He explained that he had been assigned to write my obituary, though he hoped that the story would not appear for many years. He said that my obituary, when-ever published, would necessarily include the false accusation of sex-ual misconduct made against me. I told him that the accusation was entirely made up, that I had never met my accuser, that no charges were ever brought against me and that it would be unfair to include a false and unconfirmed report of so serious a crime. He was sympa-thetic, but insisted that the accusation, even if proved false, had to be included. I subsequently received a similar call from an obituary writer from *The New York Times*. Accordingly, my obituary—a sum-mary of my life's achievements[16]—will include, perhaps feature, an entirely false and made-up accusation. It will probably not include the overwhelming documentary evidence in my accuser's own words proving that I never even met her, or the admissions by her own

---

14 Woody Allen was not charged then or since with any sexual impropriety. See also, Moses Farrow, "A Son Speaks Out", May 23 2018, available at https://mosesfarrow .blogspot.com/2018/05/a-son-speaks-out-by-moses-farrow.html.

15 His memoir was published by a different publisher and his film will be shown in the United States in late September 2020.

16 See Appendix III for a brief summary of my life achievements. For a more extensive catalogue see my book *Taking the Stand: My Life in the Law*.

lawyer that she was "wrong . . . simply wrong" in accusing me because I could not possibly have been in the places at the times she said she met me. Nor will it include a reference to the tape recording in which her best friend says that Giuffre admitted to her that she was "pressured"—her word—to falsely accuse me for money.[17]

My history will be distorted, my accomplishments will be cancelled or at least diminished, by a false accusation for which I was never charged and against which I could not formally defend. Such is the power of cancel culture: easily contrived false accusations and the current #MeToo atmosphere in which an accusation—even if demonstrably false—becomes the new truth.

Cancel culture does not include either standards or processes for determining whether a cancelling allegation is true or false. The accusation itself becomes the story, and thus becomes a part of the historical record, even if demonstrably false. Regardless of the evidence, or lack thereof, a significant percentage of readers and viewers will believe any accusation, especially against a controversial person with whose views on other matters they may disagree. This is the new reality, the new history, the new standardlessness and the new "truth" of cancel culture. Yet, because many do not understand this new phenomenon, they assume that if something appears in the media, it must be true, or at least it must have been vetted, investigated, and truth-tested before it is published. This combination—trust in what is reported by the media, coupled with the media's refusal to satisfy that trust by investigating before they publish—results in a distortion of history and truth. I will fight this distortion as long as I live, and now that I know what will be in my obituary, I will need to continue to fight it—through my children, my wife, and my friends—even after I die. This is the unjustified power of cancel culture.

One of the most morally treacherous consequences of cancel culture is its unfairness in accusing dead people, who obviously can't fight back. Many years ago I wrote a review in *The New York Times*

---

17 The indisputable evidence of my total innocence is contained in my book, *Guilt by Accusation: The Challenge of Proving Innocence in the Age of #MeToo*.

of a book on the life of the great lawyer Edward Bennett Williams. Williams had recently died, and the book's author accused him of several acts of ethical misconduct and corruption. In my review, I called this the "denial of literary due process" and wrote the following:

> I am certain that if Williams were alive and able to defend himself, he would argue that he met judges in private only to counteract the far more frequent practice—still quite prevalent, in my opinion— of prosecutors themselves meeting in private with judges. Indeed, he would probably defend the entire array of ethically questionable practices of which he was accused by pointing to egregious ethical violations routinely committed by prosecutors.
>
> This brings me to my one serious criticism of—or, more precisely, my unease about—Mr. Thomas's entire enterprise. There is something unfair, it seems to me, about disclosing Williams's heretofore unknown underside so shortly after his death. Had this book been published while Williams was still alive and healthy, I am sure he would have been able to answer some of the most serious charges against him, or at least to place them in a more positive context. Writing critically of a man who so recently died is, in effect, a denial of literary due process and of the right to confront one's accuser. . . .[18]

That was before cancel culture, which has made the denial of literary and historical due process even worse. Consider the case of one of my favorite composers and singers of Jewish Liturgy, Shlomo Carlebach, who died in 1994. Carlebach was the most influential Jewish composer of modern times. His beautiful music has been sung in synagogues around the world. I have heard it in Australia, South Africa, Russia, Canada, England, France, Italy, Israel, and other venues. He

---

18   Alan M. Dershowitz, "Winning Was Everything", *The New York Times*, December 15th, 1991. Recently, former law clerks of the deceased Stephen Reinhardt had claimed that he had sexually harassed them. Debra Cassens Weiss, "Former Clerk for Late Judge Stephen Reinhardt alleges sexual harassment and 'profane atmosphere'," *ABA Journal*, Feb. 13, 2020. Also after the documentary *Finding Neverland*—which contained no new evidence—was shown, calls were made again to cancel the late Michael Jackson. Jackson was never convicted of any crimes and denied allegations of sexual abuse.

revolutionized Jewish liturgical music. During his lifetime, he was honored and praised, though some criticized aspects of his lifestyle. He had organized a hippy-ish Jewish center in California called The House of Love and Prayer. He hugged everybody. I recall introducing him to my children back in the 1970s at a concert in the San Francisco area. He immediately grabbed me and my two children in a bear hug and told us how much he loved us. That was who he was. After his death, however, several women complained that his hugs were inappropriate and included suggestive sexuality. He was never credibly accused of any criminal behavior nor of anything that would constitute a violation of civil law. But these accusations, made at a time when Carlebach could no longer defend himself by putting them in context, were enough to have him cancelled in various venues. The Central Synagogue of New York banned his music for a year, while others cancelled him permanently.[19]

Other historic figures in the arts, business, and politics have also been posthumously cancelled. These include Kate Smith and Al Jolson. In 2019, I wrote about the cancellation of Kate Smith's beautiful rendition of "God Bless America". I acknowledged that when Kate Smith was a young, aspiring singer, she made a mistake, common in her time: she sang and recorded two songs with lyrics that today are understandably regarded as racially insensitive and offensive. She did not write the songs and she didn't continue to sing them thereafter. Many other singers, including African-American legend Paul Robeson, sang one of these songs as well. Back in the day, many lyrics reflected racial insensitivity.

Smith is now long gone, but her legacy is being attacked because of her youthful mistake. I am a Red Sox fan, so going to Yankee Stadium is, for me, a painful reminder of how often the Yankees beat the Red Sox and my beloved Brooklyn Dodgers. But I always look forward to the playing of Smith's rendition of "God Bless America". No one ever sang this Irving Berlin classic quite the way she did. But the Yankees decided to end this tradition as soon as the story of Smith's youthful

---

19 See Ben Sales, "The Synagogues that are saying #MeToo to banning Shlomo Carlebach", *The Jewish News of Northern California*, Jan 20, 2018.

indiscretion became public. The Philadelphia Flyers went even further, removing her statue from in front of their arena.

Then, I compared Smith's youthful insensitivity toward race with the mature insensitivity of *The New York Times* with regard to anti-Semitism. The international edition of *The New York Times* republished a syndicated cartoon modeled on one that appeared in Nazi Germany in 1940. The Nazi cartoon showed a stereotypical Jew leading a naive Winston Churchill. The message was clear: Jews try to control the world by leading non-Jewish world leaders to do their bidding. The *Times* cartoon was even worse. It portrayed Benjamin Netanyahu as a dog with a Star of David around his neck leading a blind President Trump, who was adorned by a kippah. The *Times* has acknowledged its mistake and insensitivity.

I am sure that Smith, were she alive today, would also have acknowledged her youthful insensitivity. The difference is that Smith has not been given a pass, while the *Times*, though embarrassed, will continue to be read by Yankee fans who will no longer hear Smith's rendition of "God Bless America."

To be sure, there are considerable differences between Smith and the *Times*. Smith was a performer whose major legacy was her acclaimed rendition of "God Bless America." But she is no longer with us.

The New York Times is not only America's newspaper of record, it is the world's newspaper of record. This means, of course, that regardless of how insensitive the *Times* has been toward Jews, their-nation state, and their leaders, there is really nothing to be done to hold *The New York Times* accountable. It will continue to publish, largely unscathed. Boycotts will not work, because their readership is too large and because many of its readers, like me, oppose boycotting newspapers and other media.

The fact that we will quickly forgive the *Times* for its far more egregious religious insensitivity should lead us to be cautious about the high dudgeon outrage some have expressed against the late Smith and in favor of cancelling her legacy. Hard as it may be to accomplish, we need a single standard of outrage, accountability, and cancellation. It should take into account many factors, most especially the time during which the offensive conduct occurred.

The lyrics sung by Smith were racist and insensitive, regardless of when they were sung, but the timing is a mitigating factor. Racial insensitivity, tragically, was the norm back then. That doesn't mean that Smith gets a complete pass, but it does mean that her entire legacy should not be destroyed by an insensitivity common to that era.

Timing is also important in assessing the accountability of *The New York Times*. It is hard to imagine a worse time than now for the *Times* to have published its anti-Semitic image, especially in its international edition. Anti-Semitism is spreading throughout Europe and in many parts of the United States, as demonstrated by murderous attacks on synagogues and on other Jewish institutions in several parts of the world. By any standard, what Smith did pales in comparison to what *The New York Times* did.

So, I called for a restoration of Smith's statute in Philadelphia and for bringing back the tradition of playing her "God Bless America". Everyone hearing that song or seeing that statute will now remember that her history is flawed by the songs she sang many years ago. So, it was right to call her out for it, but it is now also right to apply a single standard to her conduct. And under that standard, the statute gets restored and her rendition of "God Bless America" gets played.

Consider also the cancellation of Al Jolson, who was the Elvis Presley or even the Beatles of his day. He was called "the world's greatest entertainer." But he was also known as "the King of Blackface." His day was the age of vaudeville, where performing Southern-themed songs in Blackface was the norm. Was it wrong back then? Yes, but many performers did it, including Fred Astaire, Gene Autry, Ethel Barrymore, Bing Crosby, Neil Diamond, and Buster Keaton. There were few complaints back then from Black leaders. Al Jolson himself was a supporter of civil rights who helped the careers of Black performers. Yet, today, he has been largely cancelled because he performed in blackface. Others who did so even more recently have been given a pass. Cancel culture picks and chooses whom it targets without even a pretense of objective standards.

Living legends who have been cancelled include Plácido

Domingo, James Levine, Charlie Rose, Woody Allen, Linda Fairstein, Matt Lauer, Mel Gibson, Bill Cosby, Kevin Spacey, Andy Dick, Roseanne Barr, Bill O'Reilly, and Michael Richards (Kramer from *Seinfeld*). Some may deserve opprobrium, even prosecution. Some have admitted wrongdoing. Others have denied it.

There are, of course, degrees of cancellation ranging from *total*, in which the cancelled person is essentially removed from society, to *event* cancellation, in which a particular venue or organization cancels a speaker, such as Ben Shapiro, Steven Pinker, Elizabeth Loftus, or me.[20] I am thankful that the false accusations against me were made during my lifetime, when I can still fight back. Even though I am eighty-two years old and the false accusations go back nearly twenty years, I have been able to gather the documentary and other evidence that conclusively proves that I never met my accuser. Had I been dead when the accusation was made, no one else would have known where to look for the evidence of my innocence. So I am particularly sympathetic to those who have been accused and cancelled posthumously, or when they are too old or too ill to respond. They, too, might have been able to provide conclusive evidence of their innocence had they been alive or well when the accusations were made.

But, as with McCarthyism, even conclusive evidence of innocence may not be enough to cancel cancellation.

For more than a quarter century, the 92nd St. Y—the premier speaking venue for Jewish and pro-Israel speakers—invited me to discuss my books and other issues. I was told that, after Elie Wiesel, I was their most frequent and popular speaker, nearly always filling their large auditorium. Even after I was falsely accused at the end of 2014, the invitations continued, and many of my talks were transmitted to other Jewish venues around the country. There were no complaints, as far as I knew.

Then came the #MeToo movement. Although the case for my total innocence only grew stronger—my accuser's exculpatory emails were uncovered, her own lawyers admitted that she was "wrong . . .

---

20   A list of cancelled individuals appears in Appendix I.

simply wrong" to accuse me, she told her best friend she was pressured by her lawyers to falsely accuse me—the Y decided to cancel me because, although they said they knew I was innocent, they "didn't want trouble." That is precisely the excuse given by those who cancelled victims of McCarthyism back in the late 1940s and early 1950s. It is tragic and scandalous that so prominent an institution as the 92nd St Y would replicate the pernicious tactics of a bygone age.

Cancel culture combines the worst elements of self-righteousness and judgementalism. Its advocates and practitioners sit in judgment often on great people—musicians, artists, scientists—who have accomplished much good in their lives, but their actions or ideologies have offended the cancellers. Many of these who sit in judgment over whom to cancel have accomplished little in their own lives. They can't be cancelled because there's nothing to cancel. Instead, they cancel others who have accomplished far more than they have. This, in the name of some kind of false equality. Cancel culture creates its own new hierarchy in place of the hierarchy it is determined to dismantle and cancel. The new hierarchy is based on race, gender, and other statuses related to identity and "privilege."

H. Can Cancel culture be applied equally?

One true test of the virtues of a culture or concept is whether it can be applied equally, across the board, without regard to race, gender, religion, politics, ideology, or any other factors. Put another way, does the concept of cancel culture pass the "shoe on the other foot test?" Would those who advocate cancellation apply it to those with whom they agree as easily as they apply it to those with whom they disagree?

Consider for example, Malcolm X, after whom streets and buildings are named. There is considerable dispute about whether Malcolm X did any good for America, for African Americans, or for others. There is absolutely no dispute that Malcolm X was a bigot, an anti-Semite, a sexist, a criminal, and a liar. Yet there is no movement to cancel him because he is a favorite among many of those who have arrogated to themselves the role of deciding cancellations in our new cancel culture. Even Martin Luther King, whom I enormously admire and who contributed so much to so many, was a deeply flawed individual, especially in the area of sexuality, which plays such a dominant role in today's cancel culture. There is no question that he was a serial adulterer, and there are allegations that he "looked on and laughed" as a fellow minister sexually assaulted an innocent woman.[21] I hope this allegation turns out to be unfounded. We may find out when FBI tapes are scheduled to be disclosed in 2027. But, even if true, it should not cancel the positive lifelong contributions of this great man. There are also allegations against other prominent heroes of the woke generation that would easily cancel persons of the right and center. But a double standard is applied to cancellation by anonymous arbiters of the woke generation.

Does cancel culture contain elements of racial, gender, or politically based affirmative action? If so, what is the justification for that? Either a single standard is applicable to all, or the process is standardless, *ad hoc*, and based on ever-shifting values.

Among the questions raised by cancel culture is why racism and sexism are more influential in cancellations than anti-Semitism, anti-Catholicism, and other bigotries. Buildings in major universities, including Harvard, are named after virulent anti-Semites who imposed anti-Jewish quotas, as well as quotas or restrictions against other groups. These include former Harvard President A. Lawrence Lowell, former Director of Admissions Henry Pennypacker, and others. Consider the recent case of a doctor who has tweeted, "Go beat up a Zionist," "You trust the Jews, I never did," "I hope only Israelis get Ebola," and "Yahoodi[s] run the corrupt world." Despite the fact that as a resident in Brooklyn he is required to treat many Orthodox Jews, a court prevented the hospital from firing him.

---

21 Tony Allen-Mills, "FBI Tapes Reveal Martin Luther King's Affairs 'With 40 Women'", newly unearthed files claim the civil rights leader 'looked on and laughed' as a pastor friend raped a parishioner in a hotel, *The Sunday Times*, May 26, 2019.

Would the result have been the same if he had made comparably anti-Black statements? If cancellation is to become a policy, there must be debates over what standards to apply, who should apply them, what review process should be instituted, whether there is a statute of limitations, and other important issues of process. John Calhoun was cancelled by Yale—the name of the college bearing his name was changed—but other individuals, including the slave trader after whom the university itself is named, have not suffered the same fate.

One of the most daunting challenges to protect freedom of speech against the excesses of the cancel culture is the constitutional reality that cancel culture may itself be a form of First Amendment-protected expression.

I. Is Cancel Culture itself a protected form of First Amendment expression?[22]

Freedom of expression includes the right to oppose freedom of expression itself. When I was a college student and defended the rights of campus communists—both faculty and students—I was often criticized for defending the free speech rights of those who would deny free speech to others. It was an interesting moral point, especially because I was strongly anti-communist. The Stalin regime had just ended, and Communism, for me and my family, stood for repression, totalitarianism, censorship, anti-Americanism, anti-Semitism, and warmongering. But I strongly believed then, and believe now, that even those who would deny us free speech are entitled to constitutional protection for their advocacy of denial. The same is true of freedom of religion. I defend the rights of even those fundamentalists who, if they came to power, would deny other religions or atheists the right to the free exercise of their beliefs.

This is perhaps the hardest test of the true commitment to

---

22 The idea for this part of the chapter was given to me by my daughter, Ella Dershowitz.

freedom of speech: the willingness to defend those, who, if they prevailed, would deny the rest of us the basic rights, including the right to freedom of speech. The argument against free speech for free speech deniers is analogous in some respect to the argument that I often get when, as a criminal defense lawyer, I defend accused criminals who have denied others the right to live, to be free of violence, to be treated honestly, and to protect their families. A criminal defense attorney must defend the rights of those who would take rights from the rest of us. So, too, must a defender of free speech.

The repressive tactics of cancel culture would deny artists, academics, politicians, media pundits, business leaders, and others the right to a platform. Indeed, their tactic has been given the name "deplatforming." Although it does not use the power of the government as such to censor, it demands that other powerful institutions—such as the mainstream media, the academy, the church, speakers' bureaus, and others—deny those who have been cancelled the right to speak and deny their intended audiences the right to hear their views.

The reasons for cancelling someone vary considerably, but they almost always represent the values of the so-called "wokes," "progressives," and "anti-privileged." Accusations that warrant cancellation often go back as far as half a century. When it comes to the tearing down of statues and renaming of buildings, they can go back as far as the founding of our nation. They include comments (often out of context) about race, gender, and history. They also include accusations (sometimes false and unproven) regarding sexual improprieties. They include actions deemed acceptable in the time they were taken that are now disapproved of, generally for good reasons. The dead, the aged, the old, and the young are included among those subject to cancellation. Even relatives of the dead are sometimes cancelled for the sins of their fathers, grandfathers and great-grandfathers.[23] There

---

23 See James B. Stewart & Alan Rappeport, "Steven Mnuchin Tried to Save the Economy. Not Even His Family Is Happy", *The New York Times*, Aug. 30, 2020. Members of my family have been cancelled as well. And I've heard similar accounts from others.

is no due process or other mechanisms for disproving past accusations. Some are self-proving, but others are either hotly disputed or are matters of degree.

The effect of cancel culture is to shut the marketplace of ideas to those who have been cancelled and to those who wish to learn from them. Cancel culture constitutes a frontal attack on freedom of speech and due process, as I will show in the next chapter. Yet, it is constitutionally protected, at least in most of its forms and manifestations.

At its core, cancel culture is itself an expression of free speech. In my view, it is wrong speech, bad speech, dangerous speech, antilibertarian speech, and vicious speech. It is often motivated by partisan political considerations, as well as identity politics. I hate cancel culture, but, to paraphrase Voltaire, I will defend it as a constitutional right, while condemning it as a matter of morality and principle.

CHAPTER I

Cancelling Freedom of Speech for Thee, But Not for Me!

Many among the supporters of cancel culture explicitly advocate freedom of speech "for me but not for thee." They are not alone in believing that there should be selective exceptions to complete freedom of speech. That should surprise no one, because there *should* be some exceptions. But, as we shall see, most of the exceptions that are advocated tend to be self-serving, in the sense of limiting only speech that hurts or offends those pushing for the exception. Censorship of thee, but not of me!

The reality is that deep down, everybody wants to censor *something*. Human beings, no matter how committed to the abstract principle of free speech, have a deep-seated distrust of the open marketplace of ideas, especially when they themselves—or the groups to which they belong—are "victims" of the excesses of free speech. How many times have we heard a Jewish friend say, "I believe in free speech for everybody, but Nazis marching through Skokie or a Holocaust denier—that's different." Or a Black friend saying, "Of course I believe in Martin Luther King's right to parade through Cicero, Illinois, because he was a man of peace—but the Klan, with their robes and burning crosses, or allowing schoolchildren to read *Little Black Sambo* or *Huck Finn*—that's different." Or a feminist friend supporting the right to advocate and choose abortion but calling for the suppression of pornography, because it is sexist and encourages violence.

I used to conduct an experiment in my class. I would ask for a show of hands on who is against censorship. Virtually the whole class would raise their hands. Then I would start listing the exceptions and asking who would support each. A few Jewish hands go up on the Nazis. A few Black hands are raised against the Klan. Some women want to ban sexist porn. Some pacifists are willing to see *Soldier of Fortune* magazine suppressed. I then asked for other exceptions students might support. By the end of the class, it would become clear that if the students—who are against censorship in principle—were each given the power to ban just one offensive genre, there would be little left of free speech.

Several years ago, I proposed that in order to demonstrate one's *neutral* support for freedom of speech—to join what I call "The First Amendment Club"—one must attend at least one free speech rally in support of views that he or she thoroughly despises. I mean really hates! It is not enough to say, as some do about Robert Mapplethorpe's photographs, "Well, that's really not my taste, but I don't see why others who enjoy that kind of thing shouldn't be free to see it." That's easy. You must find something that really disgusts, angers, or offends you to the core. Like the bigotry of Nazis or the KKK. Go out and defend its right to be expressed. Then come and claim your First Amendment membership card. Needless to say, there are very few members of this elite club. My membership in the First Amendment Club was secured both by defense of Nazis marching through Skokie in 1977 and the position I took in 2004, when Yasser Arafat died. Palestinian students wanted to have a memorial service at which they raised the Palestinian Authority flag in Harvard Yard. The university refused permission on the ground that it only allowed the flags of countries to be flown from the mast in Harvard Yard. The Palestinian students came to me to defend their freedom of expression. I agreed to challenge the Harvard Policy, but advised them that if they were to be given permission to raise the flag, I would be there handing out leaflets telling the truth about Arafat's murderous background and how he turned down a generous peace offer that would have given the Palestinians a state. We won. They flew the flag. And I handed out leaflets describing Arafat's death as "[u]ntimely—because if he had died just five years earlier, the Palestinians might have a state." The flag and the leaflets were the perfect symbols of the marketplace of ideas at Harvard.

We all know Oliver Wendell Holmes's famous caveat that freedom of speech does not extend to falsely "shouting fire" in a crowded theater. This may well be the only jurisprudential analogy that has assumed the status of a folk argument. A prominent historian has characterized it as "the most brilliantly persuasive expression that ever came from Holmes's pen." But a careful analysis shows that it is neither brilliant nor persuasive. To the contrary, the analogy between shouting fire and core political speech is false, deceptive, and insulting. The case in which Holmes deployed that analogy upheld the criminal conviction of an opponent to World War I for handing out political leaflets and trying—mostly unsuccessfully—to persuade young men to exercise their statutory right to become conscientious objectors. That is very different from the person who shouts "Fire!" in a crowded theater, who is neither sending a political message nor inviting his listener to think about what he has said and decide what to do in a rational, calculated manner. On the contrary, the shout of "fire" is designed to force action *without* contemplation. The message "Fire!" is directed not to the mind or conscience of the listener but, rather, to his adrenaline and his feet. It is a stimulus to immediate *action*, not thoughtful reflection. It is—as Justice Holmes recognized in his follow-up sentence—the functional equivalent of "uttering words that may have all the effect of force."

Indeed, in that respect, the shout of "Fire!" is not even speech, in any meaningful sense of that term. It is a *clang* sound—the equivalent of setting off a nonverbal alarm. Had Justice Holmes been more honest about this example, he would have said that freedom of speech does not protect a person who pulls a fire alarm in the absence of a fire. But that obviously would have been irrelevant to the case at hand. The proposition that pulling an alarm is not protected speech certainly leads to the conclusion that shouting the word *fire* is also not protected. But it doesn't lead to the very different conclusion that handing out an anti-war leaflet is not within the First Amendment. The core analogy is the nonverbal alarm, and the derivative example is the verbal shout. By cleverly substituting the derivative shout for the core alarm, Holmes made it possible to analogize one set of words to another—as he could not have done if he had begun with the self-evident proposition that setting off an alarm bell is not free speech.

The analogy is thus not only inapt but also insulting. Most Americans do not respond to political rhetoric with the same kind of automatic acceptance expected of schoolchildren responding to a fire drill. The more apt analogy would be someone standing in front of a theater and urging people not to go in because he believed there may be a fire hazard. Not shouting "fire," but saying, "There may be a fire if you go in!" But Holmes could not invoke that analogy because *that* speech—as distinguished from shouting "fire"—*is* protected under the First Amendment.

Even though Holmes went much too far in his shouting fire analogy, there are other examples that most—even the strongest advocates of free speech—would accept as limitations. These include making extortionate threats, offering bribes, agreeing to conspire to commit a crime, revealing properly classified materials, or maliciously defaming another. As to other exceptions, there is reasonable debate. These include group defamation, hate speech, and showing pornography in public areas.

In this chapter, I will not be discussing close cases at the border of permissible free speech. The focus will be on core political speech and advocacy, about which the Supreme Court has been virtually unanimous over the decades. It is precisely this kind of political speech that extremists, particularly those of cancel culture, are now trying to censor. They call it "hate speech," but what constitutes hate is in the eye of the beholder, and the Supreme Court has ruled that hate speech is within the core protection of the First Amendment.

Some of this censorship occurs on private university campuses that are not governed by the First Amendment, but much of it occurs in public universities, which are prohibited from abridging constitutionally protected speech. It is this kind of core political speech that some hard-left academics and students are now claiming should be cancelled in the name of "woke," "progressive," or "identity politics" values. They seek "affirmative action" for "unprivileged" speech and "negative reaction" for speech by privileged citizens, especially white men.

Among the major problems with this new effort to justify censorship by cancellation is that it does not even purport to be politically or content neutral. It argues for cancellation and censorship only of right-wing, conservative, anti-left speech, while demanding total freedom of speech for comparable advocacy, even if hateful, directed against conservatives, right-wingers, and people of privilege. The identity of the speaker is as important as the content of the speech, though both are related.

This new approach to cancellation and censorship commits two cardinal sins: one, it restricts freedom of speech in general; and two, it prefers—privileges—some speech over other speech. It applies anything but neutral principles in its regime of cancellation and censorship because its advocates believe that neutrality in the face of inequality is a sin and that speech should be free only for those on their side and not for those with whom they disagree—for me, but not for thee. They violate what I have called "the circle of civility" test.

The circle of civility is a concept that I developed many years ago when speech codes were being proposed for university campuses. I argued that if such codes were ever to be adopted, they should be content-neutral and construct a circle of permissible speech that is not based on content, but rather on neutral "externalities." Such an approach might limit or prohibit shouting down speakers, tearing down signs, and preventing listeners from having access to venues. All of these rules would have to be applied equally, regardless of the content or the political views of the speakers or disrupters. Such an approach would involve compromises with the *first* important principle of freedom of speech: that nearly *all* speech should be permitted. But it would not compromise the *second* principle of freedom of speech: that if there are to be any restrictions, they must be content- and politically neutral.

Universities sometimes seek to justify disinviting, or refusing to invite, controversial speakers, especially conservatives, by point-ing to the expense of providing the security necessary to protect the speaker or control violent protesters. And the expense can be considerable. But denying the speaker his or her platform is not the right answer. It is not the speaker who is inciting or advocating the violence that necessitates the cost of security. The speaker is exer-cising a constitutional right. So are audience members who come to hear the speaker. And so are peaceful protesters. If the protests remain peaceful, there is no need for expensive security. It is only the threat of violent protests—which are not protected by the First Amendment—that call for expensive security. So the cost is attrib-utable to the violent protesters, not the non-violent speaker.

Moreover, canceling an event based on the cost of security encourages the use and threat of violence as a tool of censorship. If opponents of a speaker can get a speech cancelled by threatening violence and creating the need for expensive security, that becomes a tactic of the censorial hard left. We are already seeing evidence of this tactic being deployed.[1]

A similar tactic that has worked is the claim by students that the speaker makes them "feel unsafe." This contrived claim has increased dramatically since universities began to take it seriously. I'm not talking about legitimate fears to the physical safety of stu-dents. I know of no speaker who actually poses such a danger. The students who claim to "feel unsafe" are referring to ideas, not guns. But ideas are never safe, nor should they be, on university campuses. Students who are, or claim to be, frightened by hostile ideas must develop thicker skins or select a different venue for learning. They must not be allowed to use their claimed fear as a weapon to censor views they abhor. This censorial tactic, too, is used primarily by the hard-left to censor speakers of the right and center.

Consider the cancellation of Professor Ronald Sullivan and his wife as co-deans of Winthrop House at Harvard College for the "sin" of representing a controversial criminal defendant, Harvey

---

1 Katherine Mangan, "Security Costs Loom Larger in Campus Free-Speech Fights. A Lawsuit Shows Why", *The Chronicle of Higher Education*, May 24, 2018.

Weinstein. In 2019, I wrote about the argument by students that they felt unsafe with Sullivan as their dean.

> Feeling "unsafe" is the new mantra for the new McCarthyism. It is a totally phony argument not deserving of any serious consideration. Any student who feels unsafe in the presence of two distinguished lawyers doesn't belong at a university. They should leave and not force the firing of the professor. The "unsafe argument" could be used against a dean who is gay, Black, Muslim, Jewish, Republican, or libertarian. No credence should be given to the argument, especially since the students apparently did not feel "unsafe" when Sullivan was representing a convicted double murderer.

Let me now briefly describe and critique this new academic advocacy of selective censorship, based on wokeness, identity, and affirmative action.

As far back as 1965, Brandeis Professor Herbert Marcuse—a neo-Marxist "progressive"—advocated "suppression" of "regressive" opinions:

> "[I]t is possible to define the direction in which prevailing institutions, policies, opinions would have to be changed in order to improve the chance of a peace which is not identical with cold war and a little hot war, and a satisfaction of needs which does not feed on poverty, oppression, and exploitation . . . Consequently, it Is also possible to identify policies, opinions, movements which would promote this chance, and those which would do the opposite. Suppression of the regressive ones is a prerequisite for the strengthening of the progressive ones."[2]

Marcuse was wrong: prevailing over regressive opinions in the marketplace of ideas is the prerequisite for the strengthening of

---

2   Herbert Marcuse, *Repressive Tolerance* in: Robert Paul Wolff, Barrington More, Jr. and Herbert Marcuse, *A Critique of Pure Tolerance* (1969), available at https://www .marcuse.org/herbert/publicaitons/1960s/1065-repressive-tolerance-1969.pdf.

progressive ones. Current critics of freedom of speech for all, including "regressives," mirror Marcuse's "progressive" perspective and
apply it to current freedom of speech as well as academic freedom. In
a widely discussed essay in the *Harvard Crimson*, a student called for
academic "justice" instead of "freedom:"

> "The liberal obsession with "academic freedom" seems a bit mis-
> placed to me. After all, no one ever has "full freedom" in research
> and publication. Which research proposals receive funding and
> what papers are accepted for publication are always contingent on
> political priorities. The words used to articulate a research question
> can have implications for its outcome. No academic question is ever
> "free" from political realities. If our university community opposes
> racism, sexism and heterosexism, why should it put up with research
> that counters our goals simply in the name of "academic freedom"?

Instead, the student argued for what she called a standard of "justice:"

> "Instead, I would like to propose a more rigorous standard: one
> of "academic justice." When an academic community observes
> research promoting or justifying oppression, it should ensure that
> this research does not continue.
>
> The power to enforce academic justice comes from students,
> faculty, and workers organizing together to make our universities
> look as we want them to do. Two years ago, when former summer
> school instructor Subramanian Swamy published hateful commen-
> tary about Muslims in India, the Harvard community organized to
> ensure that he would not return to teach on campus.[3] I consider that

---

3   In an article in *Vox*, "I am a liberal professor, and my liberal students terrify me," a
professor from a mid-size college wrote how non-tenured faculty members will shy away
from saying anything that could be upsetting to students: "The academic job market
is brutal. Teachers who are not tenured or tenure-track faculty members have no right
to due process before being dismissed, and there's a mile-long line of applications eager
to take their place. [T]hey don't even have to be formally fired—they can just not get
rehired. In this type of environment, boat-rocking isn't just dangerous, it's suicidal, and
so teachers limit their lessons to things they know won't upset anybody." Vox.com, June
3, 2015, available at https://www.vox.com/2015/6/3/8706323/college-professor-afraid.

sort of organizing both appropriate and commendable. Perhaps it should even be applied more broadly. Does Government Professor Harvey Mansfield have the legal right to publish a book in which he claims that "to resist rape a woman needs . . . a certain lady-like modesty?" Probably. Do I think he should do that? No, and I would happily organize with other feminists on campus to stop him from publishing further sexist commentary under the authority of a Harvard faculty position. "Academic freedom" might permit such an offensive view of rape to be published; academic justice would not."[4]

Identity politics also plays a role in the demand for selective censorship. The idea that an idea is dependent on the speaker's identity—"one's location in the political and social cartography" as Professor Bettina Aptheker called it—prominently features among advocates of intersectionality, a "progressive" movement that became prominent again among the 2020 demonstrations following the death of George Floyd. As Rutgers professor Brittney Cooper, a prominent voice on Black Twitter, wrote:

"Before we have a conversation about civility, ground rules, and freedom of speech, it is incumbent upon all of us to think about the identity positions from which we make certain claims. The embodiment of scholars is central rather than incidental to their scholarship—not a constraint on academic freedom but a reasonable limit on claims to objectivity and universality. As a black woman whose research is about the black female intellectuals who came before me, I never indulge in the fantasy of noninvestment. That does not mean that scholarly distance doesn't matter. It does. But scholarly authority does not ease the embodied experiences and social investments of the very researchers who produce this work. Academic freedom and freedom of speech are never primarily about the rights of people with power. They are always about

---

4   Sandra Y. L. Korn, "The Doctrine of Academic Freedom: Let's Give Up on Academic Freedom in Favor of Justice", *The Crimson*, February 18, 2014.

the rights of people who would be silenced by those with more institutional or structural power. Having powerful white academics claim that marginalized groups—trans people, black people—are impinging on their academic freedom misses the obvious point that those groups rely on freedom of speech to be able to dissent from harmful ideas and to resist their dissemination. These dust-ups in academe are always about who has the power to shape knowledge production. So I must always stand with those who have to fight for the right to be heard.[5]

These repressive views espoused by self-proclaimed progressives would, if widely accepted and implemented, signal the death of freedom of speech and academic freedom for faculty members as well as students. "Regressive" speech by people with the wrong identities would be censored by "justice committees," whose role it would be to distinguish the politically correct speech and speakers from the politically incorrect ones. Free speech for me but not for thee would become the progressive rule, initially on campuses and eventually in institutions that come to be dominated by today's progressive students who become tomorrow's repressive leaders. Those of us who believe in maximum free speech for all must fight against this censorial mind set. We should not try to censor those who would cancel free speech "for thee," because efforts to cancel are themselves protected speech. We should offer better approaches in the marketplace of ideas, as I and others have tried to do in our books, articles, and speeches.

---

5   Brittney Cooper, "How Free Speech Works for White Academics", *The Chronicle of Higher Education*, available at https://www.chronicle.com/article/how-free-speech-works-for-white-academics

CHAPTER 2
Cancelling Due Process and Weaponizing Criminal "Justice"

Cancel culture is a direct attack on the due process of law in that it cancels people—some innocent, some guilty, some in-between—with no semblance of any process for determining the truth. This is especially true on university campuses, which have been pressured to eliminate any semblance of due process, presumption of innocence, confrontation of witnesses, or reliance on evidence instead of identity. This attack on the rule of law and basic freedoms is part of a broader phenomenon that has weaponized our justice system for ideological and partisan advantage. In order to understand fully the attack on due process in the context of cancel culture, it is important to see how partisan our justice system has become in recent years, and why our constitutional structure does not provide sufficient protections against partisan weaponization of the law, especially the criminal law.

This contrasts sharply with the criminal justice systems in most Western democracies, which have been removed from partisan politics. In Europe, Canada, Australia, Japan, and Israel, prosecutors and judges are appointed—often by non-partisan experts—rather than elected, as they are in many of our states.

Elections inevitably makes them political, because they need to raise campaign contributions and run in often-contested elections along partisan lines. Even federal judges, who are appointed by the president and confirmed by the Senate, are part of the partisan political system, as we shall see with regard to the Michael Flynn case. Chief Justice John Roberts likes to say there are no Republican or Democratic justices or judges. But cases like *Bush v. Gore*, which decided the 2000 presidential election, by a five to four vote along partisan lines, make it clear that this is more an aspiration than a reality.[1]

Indeed, presidential campaigns now promise to fill judicial seats with partisan ideological judges. The Justice Department, too, has been accused of partisanship. Presidents—from John F. Kennedy, to Ronald Reagan, to Barack Obama, to Donald Trump—have appointed loyal associates to that important role. Bill Clinton was an exception, and he rued the day he appointed Janet Reno, who was not a loyalist.

During the impeachment trial of President Bill Clinton (in which I consulted with Clinton's defense team), I wrote about the schizophrenic nature of the Justice Department, pointing out that our Attorney General—unlike officials in other democracies—plays the dual role of political advisor to the president and chief prosecutor. This produces inevitable conflicts of interests.

In other democracies, the two jobs that our Attorneys General perform are divided. There is a political office generally called the "Minister of Justice" whose job it is to advise the president or prime minister and to be loyal to the party and person in power; there is also a non-political official, generally called the "Attorney General" or the "Director of Public Prosecutors," who has no loyalty to the incumbent head of state or his party and whose sole responsibility is to investigate and prosecute in a nonpartisan manner. Prime ministers and presidents have been brought down (and upheld) by such prosecutors, without any appearance of impropriety.[2]

Our system of investigation and prosecution is unique in the

---

1   See Dershowitz, *Supreme Injustice: How the Supreme Court Hijacked Election 2000*, Oxford, 2001.

2   See Israel, where both Prime Minister Ehud Olmert and President Moshe Katsav were sentenced to prison after being successfully prosecuted by the Attorney General and State Attorney. Isabel Kershner, "Ehud Olmert, Ex-Prime Minister of Israel, Begins Prison Sentence", *New York Times*, Feb. 15, 2016; Isabel Kershner, "Ex-President of Israel Sentenced to Prison in Rape Case", *New York Times*, March 22, 2011.

democratic world. We have politicized the role of prosecutor, not only at the federal level, but in all of our states as well. Nowhere else are prosecutors (or judges) elected. Indeed, it is unthinkable in most parts of the world to have prosecutors run for office, make campaign promises, and solicit contributions. Prosecutors in other countries are civil servants who do not pander to the people's understandable wish to be safe from crime, or campaign on the promise to "be tough on crime." (Our penchant for voting on everything has reached laughable proportions in Florida, where even "public defenders" must run for office. I can only imagine what the campaign must be like.) But in the United States, prosecutors are not only elected, but the job is often a stepping stone to higher office, as evidenced by the fact that so many Senators, Congressmen, and governors who once practiced law served as prosecutors.[3] More recently, former prosecutors have been criticized for *not* being tough enough on police who have killed or injured Black individuals. This, too, has politicized the role of the prosecutor.

The polarization of justice goes beyond public prosecutors and judges. It has taken over many universities, businesses, media, and other processes for determining who is cancelled. As Justice Louis Brandeis aptly observed many years ago: "The government is the potent omnipresent teacher. For good or ill it teaches the whole people by its example." Recently, our government has provided terrible examples of pervasive injustice, politization of justice, and partisanship. It should not be surprising that these examples have taught the wrong lessons to other institutions.

A recent manifestation of the problems caused by the politization of justice and weaponization of criminal justice was the strange case of President Trump's former National Security Advisor, General Michael Flynn, who was charged with committing perjury by denying that he met with a specific Russian diplomat. The FBI recorded the meeting, and so there could be no doubt that it had taken place. Shortly after the case first broke, I argued that he had a strong defense to that charge: namely, that his lies were not material

---

3   A striking exception is Joe Biden, who was a public defender.

because the FBI questioned him for an illegitimate purpose—to give him an opportunity to lie, rather than to obtain information it did not already have.

One of the important questions posed by the Flynn case is whether a lie can be material if the FBI already had indisputable evidence of the truthful answer and asked him the question for the sole purpose of giving him an opportunity to lie.

As a civil libertarian, I believe the answer should be "No." The proper function of an FBI or a grand jury interrogation is to obtain information they do not already have, and not to create a new crime by giving the suspect the opportunity to pass or fail a morality test with criminal consequences. Related to materiality is the claim that a suspect cannot be convicted if the question was not within the proper function of the law enforcement agency that asked it.

My argument was assessed along party lines: civil libertarians who would normally be sympathetic placed their partisan allegiances above their principles and attacked my argument. Some pro-prosecution zealots supported my argument because it helped their party.

My position was attacked by Democratic partisans as lacking any basis in law. The influential legal blog, *Above the Law*, wrote an article titled "Dershowitz Invents New Materiality Standard to Protect Trump Cronies." In it, the blogger opined that "materiality does not require investigators to rely upon the false statement. This is not only well-settled, but Dershowitz's interpretation would also be a remarkably dumb standard." Others echoed these ad hominem attacks.

Well, it turns out that the issue is not "well-settled." Nor did I invent it, though I used it years ago to help win a case involving a builder who denied paying a bribe to a building inspector who recorded the bribe. In fact, two influential courts—the New York Court of Appeals, in an opinion by one of the most distinguished jurists of the twentieth century, and the D.C. district court have sided with my interpretation. (True civil libertarians should be concerned about what the law and policy should be, regardless of whether there is a precedent.)

The logic of these two courts is almost identical to the logic of my argument.

In *The People v. Tyler*, the New York court's Chief Judge, Charles Breitel, reversed a conviction for perjury of a former public official who had lied about his connection to a well-known gambler. The court reversed the perjury conviction, holding that:

> "The primary function of the Grand Jury is to uncover crimes and misconduct in public office for the purpose of prosecution . . . It is not properly a principal aim of the Grand Jury, however, to 'create' new crimes in the course of its proceedings. Thus, where a prosecutor exhibits no palpable interest in eliciting facts material to a substantive investigation of crime or official misconduct and substantially tailors his questioning to extract a false answer, a valid perjury prosecution should not lie."

The appeals court cited a district court case in D.C., which held that to interpret "materiality" more broadly would serve no proper legislative purpose. In *U.S. v. Icardi, 140 F. Supp. 383*, the court held that if "the committee is not pursuing a bona fide legislative purpose when it secures the testimony of any witness, it is not acting as a 'competent tribunal' . . . [and] extracting testimony with a view to a perjury prosecution is [not] a valid legislative purpose."

To be sure, there are differences—as there always are—between these cases and the Flynn case. But the logic of the earlier rulings is applicable to the Flynn case: namely, that a lie is not a crime unless it is material and in response to a question that is within the appropriate function of the questioner—and that it is not the proper function of law enforcement to ask questions for the purposes of giving the suspect an opportunity to lie. A judge must instruct a jury that it cannot find a defendant guilty unless it concludes beyond a reasonable doubt that the lie was material.

One can reasonably disagree on these issues, and I am ready to debate which is the better civil-liberty view. What is not acceptable is that whenever I made legal arguments that supported Republicans, my criticism was not met with considered counter-arguments, but with ad hominem attacks and with false claims that I am following some narrative of the Trump team. (In fact, it was I, not the Trump legal team, who first articulated this argument.)

These same people who criticized me would call me a hero if the 2016 election had turned out differently and this were President Hillary Clinton being investigated. They would applaud my creativity in the interest of civil liberties rather than condemning me for inventing a new argument.

It is simply wrong and dangerous to equate civil-liberty criticism of the FBI and prosecutors with support for Donald Trump.

My views on prosecutorial misconduct have been the same for fifty years. I am a liberal Democrat, and a defender of civil liberties. As such, I criticize—and will continue to criticize—government misconduct, regardless of whether it helps Republicans or Democrats, President Trump, or his opponents.

Being principled and intellectually honest means that, sometimes, your positions may conflict with your partisan preferences. For most of my critics, however, it seems that partisanship trumps their fair-weather commitment to civil liberties.

Eventually, Attorney General William Barr dismissed the case against Flynn, in part based on the arguments I had articulated. I then argued that the principles behind that correct dismissal should now be applied across the board to all similar situations and defendants, regardless of party affiliations: "If these principles were persuasive enough to warrant action in this case, they cannot rightfully be limited to one high-profile case, without lending support to the accusation, even if false, that politics could have played a role for Flynn. The Justice Department must not only be just. It must also appear to its citizens to be just."

Barr's dismissal of the charges against Flynn led to a major confrontation between the judge and the Justice Department, in which the judge—Emmet Sullivan—refused to order the case dismissed despite the decision of the Justice Department to do so.

I critiqued the judge's intervention on the pages of the *Wall*

Street Journal[4], arguing that the Constitution limits the jurisdiction of federal judges to actual cases and controversies. They may not offer advisory opinions or intrude on executive or legislative powers, except when the other branches have exercised them in an unconstitutional manner. Federal judges are umpires deciding matters about which litigants disagree. If the litigants come to an agreement, there is no controversy. The case is over.

Many judges disapprove of this limitation on their power. Not happy being umpires, they want to be commissioner of baseball. Thus courts have arrogated to themselves powers the Constitution explicitly denies them. They have invented exceptions to give themselves jurisdiction over cases in which there is no longer any controversy between the litigants.

Only the executive has the authority to prosecute or not. Implicit in that exclusive power is the sole discretion to decide whether to drop a prosecution, even if, as in this case, the court has accepted the defendant's guilty plea. Once prosecutors have agreed with the defendant that the case should be dropped, the court loses its constitutional authority to do anything but formally enter an order ending the case, because there is no longer any controversy for it to decide. There is case law, and a judge-written procedural rule, supporting Judge Sullivan's order, but that doesn't make it constitutional.

Federal judges don't have "roving commissions"—as Justice Ruth Bader Ginsburg put it[5]—to do justice as they see fit. Judge Sullivan's role doesn't include inviting outsiders with no standing or cognizable interest in the case to advise him how to decide a matter over which he has no constitutional jurisdiction. Outsiders can write op-eds criticizing the decision to drop the case. Congress can hold hearings. Professors can conduct seminars or sign open letters. But judges should not turn courtrooms into political platforms from which partisans can espouse their criticism of the administration.

The government objected to the show Judge Sullivan decided

---

4   Alan M. Dershowitz, "Judges Are Umpires, Not Ringmasters", Wall Street Journal, May 13, 2020.

5   *Shelby County v. Holder*, 570 U.S. ___ (2013) (Ginsburg, J. dissenting).

to produce in his courtroom because the decision to intrude himself into a non-controversy between the prosecutor and defendant goes beyond the Flynn case. It risks setting a precedent that would weaken the separation of powers by usurping the prosecutorial discretion the Constitution explicitly assigns to the executive branch. The United States Court of Appeals has sent the case back to Judge Sullivan, indicating that his decision can be appealed.[6]

As Justice Louis Brandeis reminded us in proposing rules of restraint on the judicial branch: "One branch of the government cannot encroach upon the domain of another, without danger." The very rule of law is being endangered by the polarization and weaponization of the criminal justice system for partisan and ideological purposes.

I cite the Flynn at length case because it is one of many that represents the trend toward partisan justice in all areas of controversy, as well as the trend away from due process and toward an ends-justify-the-means approach. This trend is most pronounced on university campuses, where due process is attacked as a weapon deployed by the privileged against the marginalized.[7]

Cancelling due process in the interests of achieving desired outcomes—whether in a specific case, as part of broader cancel culture, or as a reflection of the partisan weaponization of justice—endangers the liberties of all Americans. The rule of law and basic fairness require that whenever there is an accusation, there must be a process for resolving disputes. That is the American way. But it is not the way of cancel culture.

---

6   Spencer S. Hsu, "Michael Flynn Case Does Not Have to Be Immediately Dismissed, Appeals Court Rules", *The Washington Post*, August 31, 2020.

7   As a casebook on Community Psychology put it: "The tools of oppression are often disguised or hidden as privileges." Geraldine L. Palmer, Jesica S. Fernandez, Gordon Lee, Hana Masud, Sonja Hilson, Catalina Tang, Dominique Thomas, Latriece Clark, Bianca Guzman, and Ireri Bernai, *Introduction to Community Psychology*, available at https://press.rebus.community/introductiontocommunitypsychology/chapter/oppression -and-power/

CHAPTER 3
Cancel Culture Court

Because today's cancel culture, unlike McCarthyism and Stalinism, does not have the official imprimatur of the government, falsely cancelled victims rarely have access to the American court system. In a limited number of cases, there might be contractual rights, the right to sue for defamation, or the right to arbitrate grievances. But for the most part, since cancellation is done informally by private, often-anonymous sources, there is no legal redress. This is especially true when the accusations involve claims of sexual abuse, often many years old.

There is a close connection between cancel culture and the #MeToo movement, because many, if not most, cancellations result from accusations of sexual misconduct. Some of these accusations involve encounters between and among people that may or may not have been consensual. This is sometimes a matter of degree and perception rather than hard, objective fact. And the criteria of what constitutes permissible versus impermissible sexual contact has changed over time. In some cases, like my own, there is no matter of degree, subtle context, or changing criteria. It is simply a question of absolute truth versus absolute falsity. My case is black and white: my accuser swears she had sex with me on six or seven occasions, and I swear I never met her. There is no question or confusion or mistake; one of us is a victim, the other one is a perjurer. There is truth on one side and falsity on the other. Even so, there are barriers to judicial resolution of such conflicts. Under current law, one person can falsely accuse another of the most heinous crimes and be safe from defamation suits as long as she does it in court papers or other judicially protected documents, even if the media then publicizes it. If the accused person then publicly denies the false accusation in the media, he is not protected from a defamation lawsuit. This absurd and dangerous legal doctrine encourages the making of false accusations in judicial documents for profit or revenge. And readers are prone to believe what is contained in court documents, falsely believing that they have the imprimatur of the judiciary. Judge Jose Cabranes exposed this fallacy in an important decision of the United States Court of Appeals for the Second Circuit in a case that I brought:

> Materials submitted by parties to a court should be understood for what they are. They do not reflect the court's own findings. Rather, they are prepared by parties seeking to advance their own interests in an adversarial process. Although affidavits and depositions are offered "under penalty of perjury," it is in fact exceedingly rare for anyone to be prosecuted for perjury in a civil proceeding.[1]
>
> . . .
>
> Moreover, court filings are, in some respects, particularly susceptible to fraud. For while the threat of defamation actions may deter malicious falsehoods in standard publications, this threat is non-existent with respect to certain court filings. This is so because, under New York law [and the law of most other states], "absolute immunity from liability for defamation exists for oral or written statements made . . . in connection with a proceeding before a court." Thus although the act of filing a document with a court might be thought to lend that document additional credibility in

---

1   Ghislaine Maxwell is one of the few people who have been indicted for lying in a deposition. One of the reasons for this anomaly is that prosecutors decided not to indict her for allegedly victimizing my accuser, whose testimony they have good reason to disbelieve.

fact, allegations appearing in such documents *might be less credible* than those published elsewhere.

[T]he media does the public a profound disservice when it reports on parties' allegations uncritically . . . . Even ordinarily critical readers may take the reference to "court papers" as some sort of market of reliability. *This would be a mistake*.

We therefore urge the media to exercise restraint in covering potentially defamatory allegations, and we caution the public to read such accounts with discernment.[2]

But the media rarely exercises restraint in reporting on salacious accusations made in count-filed papers. Nor does cancel culture heed Judge Cabranes's wise caution when they cancel people on the basis of mere accusations that appear in court filings.

Because of the power of cancel culture and the lack of the power of those falsely cancelled, I am proposing the creation of a cancel culture court. This court could be established by the bar association, media organizations, or other credible groups interested in the truth. The role of the court would go beyond sexual accusations and cover anything that results in cancellation, but its primary use would probably be in resolving disputed accusations of sexual misconduct because of the close connection between cancel culture and the #MeToo movement.

The #MeToo movement does a lot of good when it exposes predatory men who have committed sexual assault against innocent women. But, as with all movements, it sometimes fails to separate the guilty from the innocent. There is no genetic predisposition for women to tell the truth or for men to lie. Both genders include some people who do both, though most women who accuse men are probably telling the truth. But what about those few men who are falsely accused by women who are exploiting the #MeToo movement for profit, revenge, or other malignant motives? As the philosopher Eric Hoffer once put it: "Every great cause begins as a movement, becomes a business, and eventually degenerates into a racket." It is important

---

2   *Brown v. Maxwell*, No. 18–2868 (2d Cir. 2019) (emphasis added).

to make sure that the #MeToo cause remains a movement and is not turned into a racket by false accusers and their lawyers looking for a quick buck.

At the moment, there is no way for a man who is falsely accused to be vindicated, short of filing lawsuits at a potential cost of millions of dollars. Accordingly, most innocent victims of #MeToo false accusers have no recourse except to issue denials, which the court of public opinion generally ignores. There should be a mechanism for innocent people who have been falsely accused to establish their innocence without having to mortgage their homes and empty their retirement accounts.

I propose, therefore, that supporters of the #MeToo movement join me in advocating the creation of an informal court, comprised of distinguished former judges, prosecutors, and defense attorneys, before whom anyone claiming to be the victim of a false accusation can bring his case. The accuser could not, of course, be compelled to participate in the one-day mini trial that this court would conduct. But if the accuser refused, the court could take that fact into consideration in rendering its judgment.

Ideally, both sides would be represented. Each would present, in four hours or so, the main evidence in support of their claims. Three possible verdicts could be rendered: guilty, not guilty, or inconclusive. The verdict would not be binding anywhere but in the court of public opinion, where the media would report on the outcome.

If such a court were to be established, I would be the first plaintiff. I doubt my accuser would appear, but I would have the opportunity to present my evidence, which the media has thus far buried. I can prove I never met her from her own emails, manuscript, and several recorded conversations with her best friend and lawyer. I have laid out my case in my book, *Guilt by Accusation: The Challenge of Proving Innocence in the Age of #MeToo* (available free on Kindle). But, despite the overwhelming evidence of my innocence and the lack of any evidence corroborating my accuser's accusation, the media continues to present my accuser as credible.

Netflix, for example, featured her in a four-part documentary series. I provided Netflix with all of my evidence—including her emails, manuscript, and recordings—and they had promised they would show them in the series in order "to tell both full sides of the story," and to present a balanced picture that would allow viewers to access her credibility. But Netflix broke their promise and presented her as a completely credible witness, while suppressing all of the evidence of her lack of credibility.

One simple example, in addition to her own emails proving that she never met me, demonstrates the unfairness of the media: my accuser accused former Vice President Al Gore and his then-wife Tipper of hobnobbing with Jeffrey Epstein on his notorious island. In exchange for $160,000, she made up this false story for a British tabloid, which published it without checking with the Gores. Had Netflix checked, they would have learned—as I learned—that the Gores didn't even know Epstein, and had never been on his island. The media should have featured this fact as an important datum in evaluating her credibility. A cancel culture or #MeToo court would hear such information as well as the other documents and recordings which the media has deep-sixed.

Another example of the media's unwillingness to spoil a salacious story by fact checking whether it is true involved the director of the Netflix series interviewing a man named Steve Scully, who worked on Jeffrey Epstein's Island until 2005. Scully vividly describes a scene that he personally witnessed in 2004, in which Prince Andrew engaged in "foreplay" with Virginia Giuffre, my false accuser, who was topless near the swimming pool—a serious allegation that Netflix could easily have checked by asking Giuffre, who is a central figure in the series, whether it is true. Had they done do, she would have told them that in 2004, when Scully claimed he saw them together on the island, she was married, living in Australia, and having babies. She had left Epstein and the United States in 2002 and could not have been on the island when Scully claimed he saw her with Prince Andrew. So either Netflix didn't bother to ask Giuffre whether the accusation was true, or they did ask her and ignored her answer.

Why such irresponsible journalism? Because to reveal the

truth—that there are blatant contradictions in the accounts of their major "witnesses"—would undercut the credibility of their one-sided narrative.

This shoddy approach to truth is typical of the entire series, and especially of the accounts of their two primary "survivor" witnesses, Virginia Giuffre and Sarah Ransome, both of whom have long and documented histories of falsely accusing prominent public figures for money. Netflix went out of its way to suppress these histories of mendacious false accusations, even though both of these witnesses have admitted "inventing," exaggerating, distorting, and outright lying about their histories and accusations. But you wouldn't know that from watching the selectively edited interviews in the series.

Consider Sarah Ransome, who is presented by Netflix as a credible person, despite the director's knowledge that Ransome has admitted making false accusation against Hillary Clinton and other prominent public officials.

Ransome says met Jeffrey Epstein when she was twenty-two years old. Years later, in the run-up to the 2016 election, she decided to go public because she believed that both candidates—Hillary Clinton and Donald Trump—were "pedophiles" who were corruptly associated with Epstein. She wrote a series of emails to a *New York Post* journalist named Maureen Callahan in which she claimed to have sex tapes of Hillary Clinton, Donald Trump, Bill Clinton, Richard Branson, and other public figures. When Callahan asked her to produce these tapes, she said they had been sent to Europe to protect them because Hillary Clinton had arranged for the CIA to kill her and she was under the protection of the KGB. Ransome urged Callahan to publish the emails containing these bizarre allegations, but Callahan refused, finding her to be non-credible. Eventually Ransome admitted to a reporter named Connie Bruck of *The New Yorker* that she had "invented"—her word—these false accusations and there were no sex tapes. She had simply made up the entire story.

Netflix was aware of this entire sordid episode, yet they put her forward as a credible source without disclosing to their viewers the indisputable evidence that she was a self-admitted liar whose word could not be trusted. Even if Netflix believed parts of her story, they were obliged to give their viewers the evidence of her documented mendacity so that they could judge for themselves whether to believe her. Instead, they deliberately suppressed it.

I know that Netflix had the evidence of Ransome's admitted lies, because I gave it to them and they promised to use it. But they deliberately censored the parts of my interview in which I provided the evidence of her lack of credibility, precisely because they didn't want their viewers to know the truth about Ransome's history of lying.

A cancel culture or #MeToo court would lend credibility to the movement. It could also be invoked by accusers when those whom they accuse deny it. The accusers would present their evidence to the court and invite the accused to challenge it. If the accused refused, then the court could consider that in its evaluation.

Consider the accusation leveled against Joe Biden by Tara Reade, which once again generated the sexist mantra of "believe women," (this time largely by Republicans), as if one gender is biologically endowed with a truth gene, and the other with a lying gene. There is absolutely no basis in science, morality, experience, or law for this bias.[3] It is no different from saying "believe Jews," "believe gays," "believe Democrats," or "believe lawyers." Generalizing about any group without an empirical basis is bigotry, pure and simple. Those who claim that "believe woman" is not bigoted because it is a positive rather than a negative attribute are simply playing word games. The necessary corollary of "believe women" is "don't believe men who deny what women accuse them of."

In the Deep South during Jim Crow, prosecutors would argue and judges would instruct juries that white witnesses were more believable than Black witnesses. These official statements were largely unnecessary because many of the members of all white juries already

---

3 Hypocritically, the hard-left understandably protests when people speculate about genetic explanations for fewer women in STEM, but not when genetic explanations are offered as to why women don't lie. This reminds me of Andrew Sullivan's quip: "Everything is environmental for the left except gays, where it's totally genetic; and everything is genetic for the right, except for gays."

believed that malignant white lie. How is this lie—that women are more believable than men—any different?

Several reasons are offered, none of which withstand critical analysis. The first is in the form of a question: why would a woman ever lie about being sexually assaulted? Making an accusation is painful and fraught with danger. A false accuser can be prosecuted for perjury or making a false report. Their reputations will be trashed, their credibility challenged, and their privacy violated. All this may be true, but insufficient to deter a false accuser who sees a pot of gold at the end of her ordeal. Since the start of the #MeToo movement, millions of dollars have been paid out to accusers. I'm sure that most of these accusations have been true, but it likely that at least some are false. A former student of mine who practices law in Hollywood has told me that discreetly accusing famous people and demanding hush money has become an industry. Even falsely accused stars are inclined to pay for the silence of their accusers rather than have the false accusation plastered all over the media. I am personally aware of several payments that were made to false accusers.

There may be other motivations beside money, including revenge, partisan political advantage, or copy-cat #MeToo-ism. The point is that there are not only *costs* to making an accusation; there may also be *benefits*. So the argument that no woman would ever accuse a man of sexual assault unless it were true is patent nonsense. Moreover, some of the "costs" are illusory. Women who falsely accuse men are rarely prosecuted for perjury, as their lawyers surely advise them. Even false accusers are often lionized by radical feminists.[4]

The second argument is that statistics prove that there are very few false accusations. But how can statistics *ever* prove that a given accusation is true unless the man confesses or the evidence is conclusive? Just because an accusation results in a conviction doesn't prove

---

4   See, for instance, the reverence given to the singer Kesha, whose song "Praying" became an anthem for the #MeToo movement. Kesha had claimed that her producer, Dr. Luke, had verbally and sexually assaulted her. She also claimed that Dr. Luke had raped Katy Perry, which Perry and Dr. Luke denied. Dr. Luke countersued Kesha for breach of contract and defamation and won in both instances. Before the legal battle, Kesha had sworn under oath that Dr. Luke never assaulted or drugged her.

that it is true, especially today, when the deck is stacked so heavily against the accused. Back in the day when convictions were rare because women were not believed, an acquittal would not prove that the accusation was false. So too today, a conviction does not prove it is true. We can't know for sure how many accusations are true and how many are false. We do know that the number of false unfounded and questionable accusations is far from trivial. Consider, again, the accusation made against me. Although my accuser has essentially admitted—in emails and a manuscript—that she never met me, and despite the fact that her own lawyer has acknowledged in a recording that she is "wrong . . . simply wrong" in accusing me, her accusation will not be counted among the false ones. Nor is it likely that she will be prosecuted for perjury, though she should be. When women like Virginia Giuffre and Sarah Ransome make up and publicize demonstrably false accusations for money, they not only hurt those they have falsely accused, they also hurt real victims of sexual abuse by casting undeserved doubt on true accounts.

The last argument is that today's women *deserve* to be believed because so many women in the past were not believed. The effort to introduce "affirmative action" into the criminal justice system is both immoral and illegal. Today's innocent defendants should not be asked to pay the price for yesterday's guilty defendants.

Every man or woman of good will should be interested in the truth, especially in the context of serious accusations of sexual or other serious misconduct. There is no downside to creating such a court and giving both sides the opportunity to present their versions of the truth. It will help the innocent, hurt the guilty, and encourage truthful accusations. It's a win-win.

CHAPTER 4

The Effect of Cancel Culture Rewriting History and Reality

The effort of cancel culture to rewrite history, not as it was, but as they wish it had been, is manifested most directly by the tearing down of statues, the renaming of buildings, and the cancelling of historic figures who have a mixed record of good and bad. Of course, all historical figures have mixed records, at least to some degree. Other than religious figures, whom history knows little about, all heroes have clay feet, and all leaders of the past and present have mixed records. Almost none would pass the tests of purity now being demanded by cancel culture.

Among recent leaders with decidedly mixed records are Mahatma Gandhi, Nelson Mandela, Franklin D. Roosevelt, Harry Truman, John, Robert, and Ted Kennedy, Winston Churchill, Martin Luther King Jr., David Ben Gurion, Menachem Begin, Oscar Schindler, and Ariel Sharon. Heroic figures of the past of every country have even more mixed records.

Several years ago, when I defended the former President of the Ukraine on charges of soliciting the murder of a critical journalist, I told him how uncomfortable I was seeing a statute of Bogdan Chmielnicki in the center of Kiev. I knew that Chmielnicki had ordered the massacre of more than 100,000 Jewish women and children, elderly, and others in the seventeenth century. He was a genocidal butcher. But the former president of the Ukraine knew him as a liberator and freedom fighter for Ukrainian nationalism. He was both. The former president promised that he would try to take down the statue and remove his image from the Ukrainian $5 bill if I won the case for him. I won the case, and he was cleared of all charges. But the statue and $5 bill remain, glorifying and honoring a Ukrainian nationalist who murdered so many innocent Jews. Nearly every country has similar heroes. Gandhi was a racist who believed that black Africans were inferior to Indians and Aryans.[1] Churchill was a colonialist. Roosevelt failed to do what he could have to help Jews survive the Holocaust. Truman ordered the bombing of Hiroshima and Nagasaki. And on and on. Consider the complex history of George Washington.

Yes, Washington, like most wealthy Virginians if his time, owned slaves—they were freed upon his death and that of his wife—but he should not be judged by that flaw alone. In addition to the great things he did for the foundation of our nation, he contributed mightily to the full equality of American Jews, which ultimately spread throughout much of the world. This part of his legacy is understated in most histories. A bit of background and context is required to fully understand what Washington did.

Most American Jews, and many non-Jews, are familiar with Washington's famous letter to the Jewish synagogue in Newport, Rhode Island on August 21, 1790. He wrote the following about the equality of Jews in our new nation:

> All possess alike liberty of conscience and immunities of citizenship. It is now no more that toleration is spoken of, as if it was by the indulgence of one class of people, that another enjoyed the exercise of their inherent natural rights. For happily the Government of the United States, which gives to bigotry no sanction, to persecution no assistance requires only that they who live under its

---

1   Gandhi was also a misogynist, see, e.g., Mayuhk Sen, "Gandhi was a Racist Who Forced Young Girls to Sleep in Bed with Him", *Vice*, December 3, 2015, available at https://www.vice.com/en_us/article/ezj3KM/handhi-was-a-racist-who-forced-young-girls-to-sleep-in-bed-with-him.

protection should demean themselves as good citizens, in giving it on all occasions their effectual support . . . . May the Children of the Stock of Abraham, who dwell in this land, continue to merit and enjoy the good will of the other Inhabitants; while every one shall sit in safety under his own vine and figtree, and there shall be none to make him afraid.

What is not widely understood is the state of the law in Britain and its colonies regarding Jews when our nation was founded. Not only did Jews lack equality in Great Britain, they also lacked equality *in the colonies*, including the American colonies. In 1753, Parliament enacted "The Jew Bill." The law provided that Jews residing in Britain or in any "of his majesties colonies in America" may become citizens "without receiving the sacrament of the Lord's supper." I own an original copy of that revolutionary law that promised to pave the way to legal equality for Jews. Before that law, Jews were anything but equal in Great Britain. Recall that they had been expelled in 1290 and returned in relatively small numbers only during the reign of Oliver Cromwell in the seventeenth century. Discrimination against them—both in law and in practice—was still rampant.

Jews celebrated their equality under the law after the passage of the 1753 "Jew Bill," but their celebration would be short-lived.

The reaction to "The Jew bill" was virulent anti-Semitism from the media, from members of Parliament, and from many British citizens. Within months, there was a movement to rescind the law, and soon thereafter it was, in fact, completely cancelled, thus leaving Jews in the unequal status they had been in before its enactment. This meant that no Jew—whether in Britain or America— could be a member of Parliament, or even a British citizen, unless they renounced their faith and adopted Christianity. Infamously, Benjamin Disraeli, who was born a Jew, could not have become a member of Parliament (in 1837) and ultimately the Prime Minister (in 1868) had he not converted to Christianity.

The American Revolution, with its Declaration of Independence, pronouncing that all men are created equal, was followed by the adoption of the Constitution, which provided that no religious test should be required to hold office "under the United States." But several states still had religious tests that excluded Jews from some of the most important benefits of citizenship.[2] That is where the status of Jews stood when Washington wrote his influential letter in 1790. It declared, in no uncertain terms, that discrimination against Jews will not be tolerated and that Jews must be treated as first-class citizens for every purpose. It was the first such broad and detailed pronouncement in the history of the world.

The Bill of Rights, adopted in 1791, further protected the free exercise of religion and precluded the federal government from establishing any form of Christianity (or any other religion) as the official religion of the government. But individual states were still free to "establish" various denominations of Christianity as their official religion. It took decades for Jews to achieve real equality all through the United States, but it might not have happened without George Washington's bold and unequivocal pronouncement.

So I, for one, will continue to celebrate Washington, while criticizing his ownership of enslaved people. No one should be surprised that our founding fathers and mothers were imperfectly great human beings.

We must come to understand the complexities of history, indeed of life. The sharp line between good and evil, preached in our churches, mosques, and synagogues is largely a fiction, especially with regard to leaders, who must often compromise principle to achieve that status.

We live in a time when it has become politically correct to destroy statues of such historic figures as Washington, Thomas Jefferson, Christopher Columbus, Andrew Jackson, and others. A lesson about such statue-tory destruction can be learned by comparing the Jewish Bible (sometimes called the Old Testament) with the Christian Bible (New Testament) and Koran. The latter two books present perfect heroes: no one could be better than Jesus, and Muslims

---

2 See Stanley Chyet, *The Political Rights of the Jews in the United States: 1776–1840*, available at http://americanjewisharchives.org/publications/journal/PDF/1958_10_01_00_chyet.pdf.

believe that Mohammed is beyond criticism. The Jewish Bible, on the other hand, presents all of its heroes as deeply flawed—that is, human. King David sinned mightily by sending Bathsheba's husband to the front line to be killed so David could marry her. Abraham lied, claiming that his wife was his sister, and came close to slaughtering his son. Joseph framed his brothers by planting a valuable item in their baggage. Moses lost his temper and struck the rock. And on and on.

I have always loved the Jewish Bible, precisely because of the imperfections of its heroes. It teaches its readers not to expect or to aspire to perfection, but only to improvement. It also judges people by their times. For example, it describes Noah as a "righteous man in his generation."

We should think about that phrase as we watch statues being promiscuously destroyed, Taliban-style, without balancing the good that imperfect humans achieved against the deeds we now correctly judge as evil. Washington and Jefferson were righteous men in their generation—a generation plagued by the unrighteousness of slavery. Although Washington freed his slaves upon his death and Jefferson tried to condemn slavery in his original draft of the Declaration of Independence, both could have done more to end the scourge of enslavement. For this they should be criticized, but their lives should also be viewed holistically, comparatively, and with a generosity of spirit. They did much good that cannot be ignored in any reckoning. That may not be the case with regard to some Confederate generals, whose statutes were provocatively placed in city centers years after the Civil War to show support for segregation. That, too, was a misuse of history. But Washington and Jefferson are different. If there is an afterlife, I can only believe they may have earned heaven, despite their hellish ownership of enslaved human beings. Should we mortals be more judgmental than the Heavenly Father? In a wonderful short story by I.L. Peretz called *Bontche Schweig*, God welcomes to heaven an obscure man who lived a poor, lonely, uncomplaining life, but without any sin—thus making him unique in heavenly or earthly history. We don't celebrate such people on earth because those who have lived sin-free lives do not become famous. When Jesus said that he who is without sin should throw the first stone at the adulteress, no one stepped forward. And if someone had, he would have become a sinner by throwing a stone at a sinning woman.

Moreover, statue-tory destruction cannot be selective if it is to be moral. Once destruction is adopted as a moral principle, it must be applied equally to all imperfect heroes who expressed or manifested bigotry against any group. Applying that egalitarian principle, the statues of anti-Catholic, anti-Jewish, anti-feminist, anti-gay, anti-immigrant, anti-Asian and anti-others must be condemned to the same fate as Washington and Jefferson. This would mean that Harvard must remove all praiseworthy references to its former President A. Lawrence Lowell, who discriminated against Catholics, Jews, Blacks, women, and other non-white protestant ethnicities. The memorials to Franklin Delano Roosevelt must come down, because he ordered the confinement of more than 100,000 Japanese-Americans based purely on racial stereotyping; he also kept closed the doors to Jewish refugees from the Holocaust. Malcolm X's name must be removed from all streets named after him because he expressed many anti-Semitic and anti-white attitudes. Thomas Edison was a bigot; so was Charles Lindberg and Henry Ford. And the FBI building should not be named after J. Edgar Hoover, who was a massive violator of civil liberties and constitutional rights.

If we demand that every acclaimed person have the merits of Jesus, we will live in a statue-free society. George Orwell predicted as much when he wrote the following in his dystopic novel *1984*:

> "Every record has been destroyed or falsified, every book rewritten, every picture has been repainted, every statue and street building has been renamed, every date has been altered. And the process is continuing day by day and minute by minute. History has stopped. Nothing exists except an endless present in which the Party is always right".

Today, it is not the "party" that is always right. It is the politically correct purists, who will surely be soon replaced by those who find imperfections in the current generation of purists, as occurred during the French, Bolshevik, and other revolutions.[3] No purist can ever be content. Pure is not a matter of degree.

We would all be better off accepting the Jewish Bible's approach to acclaim and condemnation. We should revere people who were righteous in their generation, while condemning the unrighteousness of their generation and criticizing those who could have done more to stop it. But we must not judge the imperfect heroes of the past by our own imperfect and ever-changing criteria.

Let no statue be destroyed. Let some be removed from places of honor and transported to museums, where the vices and virtues of their subjects can be explained and contextualized. Even the statue of Chmielnicki should not be shattered. It should be placed in a museum of evil-doers, alongside other villains, so that viewers can learn of their sins and crimes. But destroying statutes is like burning books, and, as Heinrich Heine prophetically warned decades before the Holocaust, "Where they burn books, they will, in the end, burn human beings too."

---

3   Hence the expression that revolutions devour their children—and sometimes their parents too.

CHAPTER 5

Cancelling Meritocracy

Cancel culture and the broader "woke" or "progressive" movement of which it is a part goes beyond cancelling individuals. It
also seeks to dismantle the entire structure of meritocracy—of judging people on the totality of their accomplishments and virtues—
and replacing it with a hierarchy based on "identity." Meritocracy
was introduced in this country precisely to replace the European
hierarchy based on nobility, bloodlines, class, religion, and other
identities. Cancel culture's effort to replace meritocracy with identity privilege is the woke mirror image of the discredited hierarchies
of the past.

The American dream, which many generations of Americans
were brought up to believe in, is that in our country, as distinguished from the old world, anyone could achieve success based on
hard work, intellect, creativity, moderation, and other commonly
accepted virtues. Here, there was no hierarchy. Anyone could make
it to the top, as evidenced by the numerous success stories, exem-
plified by the tales surrounding Horatio Alger and the many true to
life rags-to-riches biographies of American inventors, industrialists,
academics, and even presidents.

As Ruth Bader Ginsburg once asked rhetorically, "What's the
difference between a bookkeeper in the garment district and a

Supreme Court Justice?" to which she responded: "One generation." My mother, too, was a bookkeeper in the garment district. Had she been born a generation later, she, too, might have been a Justice or a lawyer. American "exceptionalism" was characterized by its meritocracy and its one-generation step from poverty and obscurity to wealth and fame.

It is true that the American dream has worked for many groups and individuals. Despite deep prejudice, bigotry, and discrimination, many children of poor immigrant Jews made it to the top by dint of hard work, saving for education and other virtues. The same is true of many immigrant communities, such as Irish Americans, Italian American, Asian Americans, Greek Americans, and others. But some groups have had greater difficulties overcoming historic and legal barriers. These include African-Americans, who suffered and still suffer from a history of enslavement and racism, Hispanic Americans, who experience language and other barriers, and women, who were not even universally enfranchised until 1920. But these groups, too, have had many rise to the top through their own efforts, sometimes aided by various types of affirmative action that recognized the need to remedy historic and continuing discrimination.

The American dream, therefore, was a selective, idealized and incomplete account of experiences of many Americans. It represented a universal aspiration achieved more by some groups and individuals than others, but not an accurate description of the many who were left behind in our "land of opportunity." Even using the term "land of opportunity" is now regarded as a microaggression by some in the cancel culture.[1]

Despite the incompleteness of this utopic aspiration, few Americans—regardless of background—challenged the very concept of the American dream and its meritocratic underpinnings.

---

1   See Jonathan Haidt and Greg Lukianoff, "The Coddling of the American Mind", *The Atlantic*, Sept. 2015 "During the 2014–2015 school year, for instance, the deans and department chairs at the ten University of California system schools were presented by administrators at faculty leader-training sessions with examples of micro aggressions. The list of offensive statements included: "America is the land of opportunity" and "I believe the most qualified person should get the job."

Many recognized that meritocracy can't succeed when educational opportunities, healthcare, housing, and other necessities of life—especially early life—are unequal. A fair race to the finish line requires that all begin at the same starting line. But until recently few, if any, in America have been against the *theory* of meritocracy: that merit—perhaps differently defined—should be a decisive factor in allocating benefits in society and selecting individuals to perform important services.

Martin Luther King summarized our aspiration in his dream:

> "That my four little children will one day live in a nation where they will not be judged by the color of their skin, but by the content of their character."

But for some among today's so called "woke," or "progressive" generation, King's dream is a nightmare that enshrines inequality. They want people to be judged not by their *individual* character or virtue, but by their *group* identity, including the color of their skin. White privilege is based largely on skin color, as is race-based affirmative action and anti-Asian racial quotas.

Efforts are underway at many universities to abolish grades in the name of equality. It's not only that grades (even based on blind grading) do not necessarily measure meritocratic achievement; it's that the very concept of meritocracy, regardless of how it is measured, is seen as inherently hierarchical, racist, sexist, and unwoke. Indeed, some now regard it as a "microaggression" to state that, "I believe the most qualified person should get the job."[2]

Symphony orchestras are now being urged to end blind auditions, in which aspiring musicians perform behind curtains to conceal gender, race, looks, and other non-musical factors. An orchestra must reflect the racial, ethnic, gender, and other identities of the nation. Diversity must prevail over musical talent, even if that results in a lowering of the standards for and qualities of musical performances. Some argue that the result of diversity will be better performances, but that

---

2 See fn. 1, *supra.*

is largely an empirical debate that could be resolved only if the comparative musical merits of blindly selected versus diversity-influenced musicians were themselves judged behind a blind screen.

Opponents of meritocracy argue that intelligence, education, achievement, and even work ethic are themselves functions of "privilege," and that privilege is rewarded enough without making it the basis for further rewards. They would distribute society's goods based on identity or "from each according to ability, to each according to need," or some close variation on that mantra. They say that hard work needs no material incentives in a truly egalitarian society and/or that hard work is its own reward and needs no further incentive. They reject the verdict of history that most societies that do not incentivize hard work with material rewards fail to get many of their members to work hard.

They also reject the verdict of experience that meritocratic evaluations are often most beneficial to the poor, the non-privileged, and those without elite contacts and influence. Blind grading—when administered fairly and without implicit bias—allows hardworking non-elites to rise to the top and surpass those with real "privilege," white or otherwise.

It is said that philosophy is often autobiography. My own philosophy of equal opportunity reflects my non-privileged upbringing— hardworking parents with no college education or contacts—and the reality that I would never have become a professor without a rigorous and credible grading system that allowed me to finish first in a law school class that included descendants of Supreme Court Justices, presidents, business tycoons, and others who were guaranteed jobs regardless of their grades. I may not have been smarter or better educated than my privileged classmates, but I worked harder and was rewarded with grades that allowed me to compete with them. Despite my grades and theirs, they still got the good jobs in the elite law firms, and I did not. But I got the clerkships and the Harvard offer, and they did not, because clerkships and professorships were granted largely on merit, whereas jobs at "elite" law firms were denied to meritorious applicants because of their religion, gender, and race.

Ruth Bader Ginsburg had the added disadvantage of being a woman at a time of rampant gender discrimination. Without grades, she, too, would not have become a law review editor, a professor, and then a Justice. Meritocracy, fairly judged, is both moral and efficient.

To be sure, there is a place for diversity over pure, blindly graded talent, and there are places where talent alone must be the criteria for selection. In legislative bodies, which are supposed to be representative, diversity should play an important role. On the athletic courts and fields, on the other hand, talent trumps diversity. If the New York Knicks roster were to mirror its fan base, there would have to be several short Jewish guys on the court and bench. No one wants to see that!

The question is not *whether* diversity should play a role; it is *what* role it should play in *which* private and public institutions. The answers should vary with the task at hand. Orchestras, surgery departments, courts of law, universities, high-tech innovators, intelligence agencies, lawyers, actors, astronauts, magicians, circus performers, opera singers, government bureaucrats, commercial pilots, fighter pilots, political candidates, TV newscasters—all these and others present different calculi on the weight to be given diversity and/or talent if they are in conflict.

Meritocracy serves several different policies, perhaps each imperfectly, but on balance probably better than its alternatives. Morally, it serves the function of generally rewarding hard work, moderation, and other virtues. Empirically, it incentivizes those virtues by rewarding those who practice them and encouraging others to do so. Pragmatically, it seeks to protect those who rely on meritocracy to produce the most capable providers of important services.

As to this last issue, we want to be sure that our brain surgeons are selected solely on the basis of factors that are relevant to their ability to save our lives and not on factors that may serve other societal interests. If some are selected on the latter basis, we have a right to that information in selecting a surgeon. Some patients may decide to use a surgeon who was selected by criteria other than merit, but others should have the right to place their own safety over other values in life-and-death situations. I have always said I prefer ugly and uncharming doctors who must have made it to the top based on their medical skills alone.

Reasonable people may disagree about what the factors are that determine medical excellence, but few would select a brain surgeon who was less qualified than another.[3] The same would be true of a commercial pilot or a combat-jet navigator. The opposite might be true of a legislator whose identity may be at least as important as his or her talent in enacting legislation.

With regard to diversity, Ruth Bader Ginsburg was once asked, "When will there be enough women on the Supreme Court?" She responded, "When there are nine." Although this was a quip, it does reflect the reality of what some people regard as diversity: more of us and less of them, even if the more of us reduces actual diversity. For many, diversity is simply a means for increasing the number of people with whom they identify. I have never heard an African American leader demand diversity among players in the National Basketball Association. (There have been demands for more diversity among owners and coaches.) Nor have I heard many progressive or woke zealots seek more Republicans, Christian fundamentalists, gun advocates, or opponents of affirmative action to diversify student bodies or faculties at universities. The demand for diversity is often a euphemism for more of those the demanders want and fewer of those they don't want. In practice, the kind of diversity demanded by the hard-left often reduces rather than increases intellectual, political, religious, and ideological differences.

The effect of cancel culture and its effort to cancel the legacies of so many who achieved so much by meritocracy is an assault on due process and other constitutional values. Its dangerous effort to substitute identity for meritocracy is a direct attack on Martin Luther King's American dream.

---

3   A leading Palestinian politician chose to have a serious operation in Europe rather than in Israel, although the Israeli surgeon was reportedly more skilled than the European. He feared that if he were to die at the hands of the Israeli, many of his countrymen would suspect foul play.

CHAPTER 6
Cancel Culture Cancels Israel

Cancel culture does not limit itself to cancelling individuals with whose policies or actions it disagrees. Many in cancel culture seek to cancel the nation-state of the Jewish people, not only because they oppose its policies and actions, but because they oppose its very existence. Cancellation of Israel is manifested by "maps" that literally erase Israel and substitute Palestine.[1]

In order to become a full member of the "woke" generation and its culture, an aspirant must stand against the existence of Israel and Zionism. Zionism—which simply supports the *existence* of Israel as the nation-state of the Jewish people, not necessarily all of its *policies* and actions—is seen as incompatible with woke values, identities, and organizations, such as Black Lives Matter, feminism, environmentalism, and other left-wing causes. Israel is seen as the national manifestation of "white privilege," despite its multi-racial, ethnic, and religious diversity. Zionism is seen as being incompatible with feminism.[2]

One of the most visible spokespersons for current "progressives"—Peter Beinart—has called for the cancellation of Israel as

---

1   Palestinian Authority, Palestinian Maps Omitting Israel https://www.jewishvirtual
library.org/palestinian-maps-omitting-israel
2   See Emily Shire, "Does Feminism Have Room for Zionists", *The New York Times*,
March 7, 2017.

the nation-state of the Jewish people and the substitution of a single bi-national, bi-religious state in what is now Israel, the West Bank, and Gaza.[3] The Jewish population in what is now Israel would then be gathered into some sort of "homeland" within the new nation. But Beinart is woefully ignorant of previous attempts to create or maintain bi-national or bi-religious states. He ignores the lessons of history surrounding the former Yugoslavia—Tito's failed effort to create a single artificial nation from different ethnicities and religions—which ended in genocide, tragedy, and its breakup into several states now living in relative peace. He omits any mention of Lebanon—a failed experiment in sharing power between Muslims and Christians—which ended with the expulsion of much of the Christian population. He writes as if Hindu India still includes Muslim Pakistan, instead of having been divided after considerable bloodshed and divisiveness. He focuses instead on two countries, Northern Ireland and South Africa, which bear little relationship to current day Israel and Palestine. Northern Ireland is a country whose population is ethnically similar, with only religious differences at a time when religion is playing a far less important role in the lives of many secular Northern Irelanders. South Africa was a country in which a tiny minority of whites dominated a large majority of Blacks, and is now a dominantly Black nation.

Israel and Palestine are totally different. The population of Israel is a mixture of Ashkenazi and Sephardic Jews, Muslims, Christians, and others. The West Bank and Gaza are comprised almost exclusively of Muslim Arabs. There used to be a mixture of Muslims and Christians, but many Christians have been forced out. The combined population of the West bank and Gaza is close in numbers to the Jewish population of Israel. If Israel were to be cancelled as the nation state of the Jewish people—as Beinart advocates—and become a Jewish "homeland" in a single bi-national, bi-religious state, a demographic war would become inevitable, in which Jews and Muslims would compete to become a majority. As soon as a Muslim majority materialized, the Jewish "homeland" would become precisely the kind of "Bantustan" that Beinart has railed against in the context of South Africa. Or it

---

3   Beinart, "I No Longer Believe In A Jewish State," *New York Times*, July 8th, 2020.

would become a new "ghetto," reminiscent of the old Jewish ghettos of Europe. The Jewish minority would be ruled by the Muslim majority, even if the Jews were given some autonomy. Their protection would be largely in the hands of the Muslim majority, many of whom believe there is no place for a Jewish entity anywhere in the area.

It was precisely this fear and experience that led to the creation of political Zionism in the nineteenth century. Theodor Herzl and others experienced the anti-Semitism of Europe and the inability of the Jewish minority to protect itself against pogroms and discrimination. Placing the safety of Israel's Jewish population in the hands of a potentially hostile Muslim majority would be an invitation to possible genocide.

Beinart is insistent that today's Israelis and Jews must ignore the lessons of the past, including the ghettos, pogroms, and the Holocaust. But those who ignore the history of the past are destined to repeat it. And Jews cannot afford to see a repetition of their tragic past.

Beinart never discusses the issue of who would control the armed forces, and most particularly Israel's nuclear arsenal, under a bi-national and bi-religious state in which the Jews merely had a homeland. States have armies; homelands do not. Recall that the current Palestinian constitution demands that a Palestinian state be an Islamic nation bound by Sharia Law. Even if the Palestinian majority state would allow the Jewish homeland to have its own domestic laws, the state itself, with its Muslim majority, would presumably control the armed forces. This would create yet another Islamic state, among the many that currently exist, but this one would have a nuclear arsenal. Nor would a Palestinian majority allow persecuted Jews from around the world to seek asylum, as they can do today under the law of return. Instead, the Palestinian state would enact its own law of return that would allow millions of exiles to "return" and assure a permanent Muslim supermajority.

Beinart's article is maliciously deceptive in that it places the blame for the absence of a two-state solution largely on Israel, willfully omitting Israel's willingness over many decades to accept a Palestinian state. In 1937 and 1938, the Peale Commission recommended the division of mandatory Palestine into Jewish and Arab states. The proposed Jewish state was far smaller and less contiguous than the state offered to the Palestinian Arabs. The Jews reluctantly accepted the two-state offer, while the Arabs adamantly rejected it, saying that they wanted there not to be a Jewish state more than they wanted a state of their own. The same was true in 1947 and 1948, when the United Nations partitioned mandatory Palestine into two states for two peoples. The Jews once again accepted that proposal, while the Arabs rejected it and went to war against Israel. In 1967, the Israelis accepted Security Council Resolution 242, which would have returned the vast majority of conquered lands to the Arabs. The Arabs convened in Khartoum and issued their three famous no's: no peace, no recognition, no negotiations. In 2000 and 2001, President Clinton and Israeli Prime Minister Ehud Barak offered the Palestinians a state on more than 95% of the disputed territories. Yasser Arafat rejected it and began an intifada that killed 4000 people. In 2008, Israel's Prime Minister Olmert offered the Palestinians even more. You wouldn't know any of this from reading Beinart's biased and deceptive "history." Beinart willfully omits these facts because they don't serve his biased narrative. He claims to know what is best for both Israelis and Palestinians, without regard to what *they* want. He ignores the wishes of those who have the most at stake.

Beinart arrogantly rejects democracy and the polls that show that most Israelis and Palestinians are opposed to his one-state solution. He has it exactly backwards when he argues that only "Palestinian and Jewish hardliners" resist his one-state solution. It is only hardliners who want one state: many Muslim hardliners want one Palestinian state "from the river to the sea," and some Jewish hardliners want a Jewish state in all of biblical Israel.

Beinart rejects the democratic preferences of most Israelis and Palestinians for two separate states.

Beinart's attempt to destroy the nation-state of the Jewish people would undo decades of sacrifice and hard work by Zionists since the middle of the nineteenth century. Despite its imperfections, Israel is a wonder of the world. It has given more to humankind—scientifically, medically, technologically, literarily, and in so many other areas—in the seventy-two years of its existence than any country of

the history of the world. No nation faced with the threats comparable to those faced by Israel—including terrorism, rocket, and terror
tunnels attacks, as well as Iranian aggression—has ever had a better
record of human rights, compliance with the rule of law, and con-
cern for enemy civilians than Israel.

In a world with so many Islamic, Christian, and other religious
and national states, why does Beinart believe there is no room for
one nation-state of the Jewish people capable of protecting its citizens from aggression, capable of welcoming oppressed Jews from
around the world, and dedicated to equal rights for all of its citizens?

Beinart's nasty and ignorant attempt to cancel Israel belongs
in the wastebasket of history, along with the rest of cancel culture.
He has lost all claim to speak for any segment of the pro-Israel and
Jewish community by siding with those who would cancel the existence of the only nation-state of the Jewish people.

Fortunately, Beinart's anti-Israel efforts to cancel Israel are likely
to be accepted only by anti-Israel extremists and by left-wing Jews
who are embarrassed by Israel's strength and determination to protect the Jewish people against experiencing a repeat of their tragic
history. It was this history that led to the widespread acceptance of
Zionism and the formation of the democratic nation-state of the
Jewish people. The citizens of Israel—both Jewish and Muslim—
will be the ones to decide on the appropriate solution to the Arab-
Israeli conflict. They overwhelmingly support a two-state solution,
and they overwhelmingly reject Beinart's dangerous solution. If the
Palestinians want to have input into these decisions, they will have
to come to the table and negotiate. Their fate, and the fate of their
Israeli neighbors, will not be decided on the op-ed pages of *The New
York Times*, in the classrooms of anti-Israel professors, or by protests
in European capitals. It will be decided on the ground by negotiations between the Israelis and the Palestinians.

It will also be influenced by the attitudes and actions of other
Arab nations in the region, especially Sunni nations, such as the
United Arab Emirates.

The agreement by the United Arab Emirates (UAE) to normal-
ize relations with Israel bodes well for the future of Israel and the

dangerous region in which it lives. It was not the first such agreement—there were peace treaties with Egypt (1979) and Jordan (1994)—and it will probably not be the last. It is likely, though not certain, that other Gulf nations may follow. Even the president of Lebanon has "hinted at the possibility of peace talks with Israel," despite objections from Hezbollah.

Although the Palestinian leadership opposed the deal—it always opposes everything—it, too, may benefit from it. The UAE will press for a two-state solution, and its voice will be more influential both in the United States and in Israel. A two-state solution that assures Israel's security would require a demilitarized Palestine with an Israeli military presence in the Jordan Valley and territorial swaps that keep the current large settlement blocks as part of Israel. This would allow for a contiguous, viable Palestinian state that could thrive if it maintained peace with Israel. The Palestinians could secure such a state if they were to agree to negotiate with Israel over the current Trump plan that is now on the table—a plan I worked on over the past several years.

The UAE deal makes clear that the Palestinian leadership no longer has a veto on the actions and attitudes of its Arab neighbors, who will do what it is in their own best interests. It has also become clear that strengthening ties with the militarily, technologically, and economically powerful Israel is the best protection against the dangers posed by an Iran that for decades has been seeking to have its own deliverable nuclear-weapons capability.

Most United States Democratic Party leaders, including presidential candidate Joe Biden and his vice-presidential pick, Kamala Harris, have praised the deal. One of the very few prominent Americans who belittled the agreement was Ben Rhodes, a foreign policy adviser to former President Barack Obama, who was instrumental in making the dangerous deal with Iran that essentially green-lighted the mullahs' quest for a nuclear arsenal.[4]

Ironically and perversely, it was the pro-Iran policy of Obama and

---

4   Peter Beinart retweeted a Tweet that claims that the deal was "meant to . . . avert gaze away from the occupation." Seth Frantzman, "Why aren't pro-peace voices celebrating the UAE-Israel Deal", *Jerusalem Post*, August 30, 2020.

Rhodes that contributed to the fear that drove the UAE closer to Israel. The Emirates know that Israel will never allow Iran to develop or acquire nuclear weapons, no matter what it takes to stop them. For the rest of the world—including the United States—a nuclear Iran is a regional diplomatic problem. For Israel, it is an existential danger. For the Gulf States, it poses a serious threat to their regimes.

The deal, however, is more than "the enemy of my enemy is my friend." The UAE will derive many benefits from closer relationships with the Middle East's most stable and advanced country. These include economic and technological partnerships, military and intelligence sharing, mutual tourism, and better relationships with the United States and much of the rest of the world.

The deal also demonstrates how quickly changes occur in this volatile part of the globe. It was only a few decades ago when Israel's strongest allies were Iran and Turkey, and its most intractable enemies were Egypt, Jordan, and the Gulf States. Now the reverse is true. The only constant constructive element in the region is a democratic Israel, with its close ties to the United States.

The other constant—but a destructive one—has been the Palestinian leadership. They constantly say no to everything that involves normalization with Israel. This naysaying approach has been constant from the 1930s to the present, with their refusal even to negotiate over the Trump peace deal. As Abba Eban once put it: The Palestinians can't take yes for an answer and never miss an opportunity to miss an opportunity.

But the UAE can take yes and doesn't miss opportunities. The rest of the Arab world should follow. Maybe then the Palestinian leadership will realize that they, too, should sit down and negotiate a full peace with the nation-state of the Jewish people.

Israel will not be cancelled, regardless of what Beinart and his fellow woke progressives may desire. It is here to stay and it will remain the nation-state of the Jewish people with equal rights for all of its citizens, of whatever religion or non-religion.

CHAPTER 7
Cancelling Anti-Semitism in Black Lives Matter Platform

B lack Lives Matter has become an ally of cancel culture in that anyone who challenges the concept risks cancellation. People have been cancelled for saying or tweeting "All Lives Matter" or "Blue Lives Matter."[1] Leslie Neal-Boylan, Dean of Nursing at UMASS Lowell, sent an email to students and staff addressing the George Floyd protests. She wrote: "I despair for our future as a nation if we do not stand up against violence against anyone. Black Lives Matter, but also, Everyone's Life Matters." A student shared the statement on Twitter and Neal-Boylan was subsequently fired.[2] But the Black Lives Matter organization itself has engaged in bigoted rhetoric which, had it been uttered by organizations with a different identity, might have resulted in its cancellation.

It is a tragedy that the Black Lives Matter organization—which has done so much good in raising awareness of police abuses—has moved away from its central mission and has declared war against the nation-state of the Jewish people. In its "platform," more than

---

1   Grant Napear was fired by KTHK Sports 1140 and resigned from his position as a TV announcer for the Sacramento Kings after a former Sacramento Kings player asked his opinion on Black Lives Matter over Twitter. Napear responded, "All lives matter . . . Every single one!!!"

2   foxnews.com

sixty groups that form the core of the Black Lives Matter movement went out of their way to single out one foreign nation to accuse of genocide and apartheid.

No, it wasn't the Syrian government, which has killed tens of thousands of innocent people with barrel bombs, chemicals, and gas. Nor was it Saudi Arabia, which openly practices gender and religious apartheid. It wasn't Iran, which hangs gays and murders dissidents. It wasn't China, which has occupied Tibet for more than half a century and confined thousands of Muslims. And it wasn't Turkey, which has imprisoned journalists, judges, and academics. Finally, it wasn't any of the many countries, such as Venezuela, Mexico, or India,[3] where police abuse against innocent people run rampant and largely unchecked. Nor was it the Hamas-controlled Gaza Strip, where the police are a law unto themselves who act as judge, jury, and executioner of those whose politics or religious practices they disapprove.

It was only Israel, the nation-state of the Jewish people and the only democracy in the Middle East. The platform accuses the US of being "complicit in the genocide taking place against the Palestinian people" by providing aid to "an apartheid state."

To be sure, Black Lives Matter is not a monolithic organization. It is a movement comprising numerous groups. Many of its supporters have no idea what the platform says. They cannot be faulted for supporting the movement or its basic mission. But the platform is the closest thing to a formal declaration of principles by the Black Lives Matter organization. It sets out the organization's policies. The genocide paragraph may well have been injected by radicals who are not representative of the mainstream. But now that it has officially been published, all decent supporters of Black Lives Matter—and there are many—must demand its removal.

Criticizing Israel is not anti-Semitic. Like other democracies,

---

3   See Jeffrey Gettleman & Sameer Yasir, "Hundreds of Police Killings in India but No Mass Protests", *The New York Times*, Aug. 20, 2020. The argument that Israel is singled out because it receives considerable foreign and military aid from the U.S. is belied by the fact that India, too—as well as other countries with police abuse— receives U.S. aid. Even if the U.S. were to end its aid to Israel, the radical left would not end its singular criticism of the nation-state of the Jewish people.

including our own, it has faults. Criticizing Israel's settlement and occupation policies is fair game. But singling Israel out and falsely accusing it of "genocide" can be explained in no other way than blatant hatred of Jews and their state. As *New York Times* columnist Tom Friedman aptly put it:

> Criticizing Israel is not anti-Semitic, and saying so is vile. But singling out Israel for opprobrium and international sanction—out of all proportion to any other party in the Middle East—is anti-Semitic, and not saying so is dishonest.

By that standard, the Black Lives Matter platform is anti-Semitic and to say otherwise is dishonest. In addition to being anti-Semitic, it is also anti-historic.

In defending its citizens against terrorism since before its establishment as a state in 1948, Israel has killed fewer Palestinians than did Jordan and Syria in two much shorter wars. The relatively low number of civilian deaths caused by Israeli self-defense measures over the past three-quarters of a century compares favorably to the number of civilian deaths in other conflicts. This is because, as Colonel Richard Kemp, former commander of British Forces in Afghanistan, put it: There has been "no time in the history of warfare when an Army has made more efforts to reduce civilian casualties . . . than [the Israel Defense Forces]." Though Kemp was specifically referring to the wars in the Gaza Strip—which are also the apparent focus of the Black Lives Matter Platform—his conclusion is applicable to all wars Israel has fought.

Genocide means the deliberate extermination of a race, such as done by Nazi Germany to Jews and Sinti and Roma, or by the Hutu against the Tutsi in Rwanda, or by the Turks against the Armenians. It has no application to deaths caused by self-defense measures taken to protect citizens against terrorism. If it did, nearly every warring country would be guilty. To falsely accuse Israel of "genocide"—the worst crime of all, and the crime whose very name was coined to describe the systematic murder of six million Jews—is anti-Semitic, pure and simple. There is no getting around that verity.

Defenders of Black Lives Matter argue that the inclusion of this critique against Israel in not anti-Semitic; it is merely anti-Zionist. That is false. As a law professor for fifty years, I frequently used "hypothetical cases"—the students called them "hypos"—to deepen the analysis of a problem. So please consider the following hypo: Imagine a world in which there was only one Black African nation—a nation built largely by previously enslaved Black men and women. Imagine further that this singular Black nation had a good record on the environment, on gay rights, on gender equality, on human rights, and on defending itself against attack from predominantly white nations. But, as with all nations, the Black nation was far from perfect. It had its flaws and imperfections.

Now imagine further that do-gooder organizations in America and around the world were to single out the Black nation for unique condemnation. For example, imagine that an environmental group or a gay-rights group were to publish a platform in which it criticized the environmental or gay-rights policies of its own nation, but then went out of its way to single out only one other nation—the Black nation—from among all the other polluters and homophobic countries of the world?

Would anyone hesitate to describe the singling out of the world's only Black nation for unique condemnations as an act of bigotry, motivated by anti-Black racism? If that is the case, how is it different when Black Lives Matter singles out the only nation-state of the Jewish people for unique and undeserved condemnation? Is not the application of a double standard based on religion as bad as a double standard based on race?

I'm reminded of a story involving the anti-Semitic former President of Harvard, A. Lawrence Lowell, who justified anti-Jewish quotas by asserting that "Jews cheat." When a distinguished alumnus pointed out that non-Jews cheat as well, Lowell responded, "You're changing the subject; we are talking about Jews." Well, you can't talk only about Jews when discussing cheating, and you can't talk only about the nation-state of the Jewish people when you are discussing human-rights violations.

Criticizing Israel for its imperfections is not only fair, it is desirable. But only when it is based on a single standard of comparison with other nations of the world. Condemning the nation-state of the Jewish people alone, in a world with far greater offenders, cannot be justified by any moral principle. It is anti-Semitic, pure and simple. And the Black Lives matter platform is guilty of the serious sin and crime of anti-Semitism.

Until and unless Black Lives Matter removes this blood libel from its platform and renounces it, no decent person—black, white, or of any other racial or ethnic background—should have anything to do with it, as an organization.[4] We should continue to fight against police abuses by supporting other organizations or forming new ones. But we must not become complicit in the promotion of anti-Semitism just because we agree with the rest of the Black Lives Matter program.

To support an organization or movement that promotes anti-Semitism because it also supports good causes is the beginning of the road to accepting racism. Many racist groups have also promoted causes that deserve support. The Ku Klux Klan organized summer camps for working-class families, while advocating violence against blacks. The Black Panthers had breakfast programs for inner-city children, while advocating violence against whites. Henry Ford built good cars while promoting rabid anti-Semitism. And Mussolini made the trains run on time.

There must be zero tolerance for anti-Semitism, regardless of the race, religion, gender, or sexual orientation of the bigots who promote, practice, or are complicit with it. Being on the right side of one racial issue does not give one a license to be on the wrong side of the oldest bigotry.

To give Black Lives Matter a pass on its anti-Jewish bigotry would be to engage in reverse racism. Black anti-Semitism is as inexcusable as white anti-Semitism or white racism. There can be no double standard when it comes to bigotry.

---

4   The Black Lives Matter statement says "#BlackLivesMatter is a network predicated on Black self-determination, and BLM Chapters reserve the right to limit participation based on this principle." Their website also describes our society as a "hetero-patriarchal society," in which "normality [is] defined by 'white supremacy.'"

I write this critique both in sorrow and in anger. In sorrow, because I support the goals of the Black Lives Matter movement—I have long been involved in efforts to expose and prevent police abuses— and worry that this obnoxious and divisionary platform plank may destroy its credibility with regard to police abuse in America by promoting deliberate lies about Israel. It is also alienating Jewish and other supporters who could help them achieve their goals here at home—as many such individuals have historically done in actively supporting all aspects of the civil-rights movement.

I write it in anger because there is never an excuse for bigotry and for promoting blood libels against the Jewish people and their state. It must stop. And those who engage in it must be called out for condemnation.

I also write in fear, because the Black Lives Matter organization has become so powerful, pervasive, and influential, I fear that anything it says in its platform may come to be believed by many of its supporters, and if the genocide lies came to be believed by large number of decent, but naïve people, it could endanger Israel, Zionists, and Jews.

Black Lives Matter should cancel the portions of the platform that falsely accuse Israel of genocide and apartheid. If it does not, it risks ending in the dustbin of history, along with other discredited bigoted groups.

It would be sad if the good work done by Black Lives Matter were now to be sidetracked by the mendacious and irrelevant accusation of "genocide" and "apartheid" against one foreign democracy—Israel.

Here is one instance where cancellation could produce a positive outcome: Black Lives Matter should cancel its anti-Semitic, mendacious, and singular attack on the nation-state of the Jewish people. If it refuses, then people of good will should cancel Black Lives Matter as an *organization*, but not as a *concept*, and continue to support racial justice through other, non-bigoted organizations.

Some may argue that the anti-Semitic platform is just words, but words matter and have an impact on actions. The bigoted words in the Black Lives Matter platform may well have led to the bigoted actions of some protestors. Following the inexcusable killing of

George Floyd, righteous protests arose across the world. Tragically, however, some protestors, especially on the hard-left, tried to exploit the protests to level their typical baseless charges against Israel. Signs and chants at several protests have either tried to blame Israel—falsely, as it turns out—for training the policemen who are responsible for Floyd's death, or to compare police brutality in America with legitimate efforts by the Israel military to prevent acts of terrorism against civilians. A cartoon that is being circulated on social media shows an American policeman with his knee on the neck of an African American man and an Israeli soldier with his knee on the neck of a Palestinian man. The policeman and soldier are embracing. The caption above reads: "Black Lives Matter," though there is no evidence that the organization—notwithstanding its platform—has anything to do with this bigoted cartoon. A painting of George Floyd wearing a Palestinian keffiye is also being circulated. Anti-Israel graffiti—"F . . . K Israel," "free Palestine"—has been sprayed on synagogue walls in Los Angeles during anti-racist demonstrations.

This "blame it on Israel" or "blame it on the Jews" bigotry is common throughout the world at demonstrations for legitimate causes that are unrelated to the Mid-East. Anti-Israel extremists from the hard-left try to promote the intersectionalist propaganda that all the evils of the world are produced by privileged white democracies, such as the United States and Israel. Islamic extremists—who are hard to classify as left or right—use any excuse to demonize Israel. Anti-Semitic extremists from the hard-right have always tried to blame the Jews for all of the world's evils. An old Polish expression summarized it well: "If there is trouble in the world, the Jews must be behind it." Today, that has been expanded by the hard-left and Islamic extremists to include the nation-state of the Jewish people among those who cause the world's problems, ranging from capitalism, to destruction of the environment, to police violence. British Labor parliamentarian Clare Short has said that Israel is the cause of "global warming" as well as "bitter division and violence in the world" and may one day be the cause of "the world ending."

Historically, the Jews have always been caught between the black of Fascism and the red of Communism. This was true in the 1920s and 1930s in Europe, and there is a danger that it could now manifest itself during this time of extremism, when bigots on both sides are prepared to scapegoat the Jews and their nation state.

Those of us who are both Jewish and liberal—who support Israel and oppose unjustified police violence—must be willing to participate and encourage legitimate protests against police violence, such as that caught on video in the Floyd case. We must stand up and be heard in condemnation of such violations, but we must stand up and be heard against those who would exploit tragedies to foment violence against Jews and the nation-state of the Jewish people.

We should not generalize: the vast majority of protestors are focused on the injustices of police misconduct. But we cannot ignore those—even if they are relatively few in number—who would turn these protests into bigoted attacks against Israel. Bigotry unanswered grows in size and intensity.

Silence is not an option in the face of any injustice. Black lives matter greatly; so do Palestinian lives; so do Jewish and Israeli lives. We must not be afraid of being criticized for condemning bigotry on all sides. As the great sage Hillel put it 2000 years ago, "If I am not for myself, who will be for me? If I am for myself, alone, what am I?" He ended his statement with a call to action: "And if not now, when?"

Now is the time to protest the injustice of the deaths of George Floyd and other African American men and women who have been unjustly targeted by overzealous, and often racist, police. But now is also the time to speak out against those who would hijack this tragic history to manifest the oldest continuing prejudice known to mankind, namely anti-Semitism.

The Black Lives Matter organization would do much good if it cancelled its anti-Semitic platform reference to Israel and if it did not allow its righteous protests against racial injustice in the United States to be hijacked by anti-Israel bigots.

Addendum

As this book was going to press, the *Jerusalem Post* reported that the movement for Black Lives is "convening a Black National Convention, where it's going to unveil another policy platform" and that "a ten-page summary of the 2020 platform . . . contains no mention of Israel. . . ." A representative of the movement "could not say for certain whether the full platform would include any mention of Israel," but "losing the language entirely could make Black Lives Matter vulnerable to criticism from pro-Palestinian activists who are often in coalition with anti-racist groups."[5] It would be a positive development if the new platform cancelled the earlier anti-Semitic one and would demonstrate that protests against anti-Semitism sometimes work.

---

5   Ben Sales, "New Movement for Black Lives platform contains no mention of Israel", *Jerusalem Post*, August 29, 2020.

CHAPTER 8
Cancelling The Bible, Which Commands Personal Justice, Not the Double Standard of "Identity Justice"

Cancel culture violates not only constitutional norms that go back two-and-a-quarter centuries, but also biblical norms that go back three millennia.

The Bible had a great deal to say about cancel culture, justice, due process, and false accusations that are worth heeding today. In Chapter 4, I wrote about the Bible's approach to judging imperfect people who were "righteous" in their generation, but not by current standards. In this chapter, I discuss the Bible's approach to justice and due process.

I recently celebrated the sixty-ninth anniversary of my Bar Mitzvah. To commemorate it, my son videotaped me chanting from the same Torah portion I chanted in 1951 in Brooklyn. The words I intoned were written three thousand years ago. And yet not a single revision is required to make them relevant to today's world.

My portion begins with a command to the Israelites to "appoint judges and magistrates in all your cities." The judges are then commanded not to pervert justice by showing favoritism or taking bribes, which "blinds the eyes of the wise and perverts just words." Then comes the central command, perhaps of the entire Torah: "Justice, Justice must you pursue." Actually, the word pursue is not as strong in the English as it is in the Hebrew. The Hebrew word, *tirdof*, literally means to chase or run after. It is as if God was telling his people that the quest for justice never stays won. It must always be actively pursued. No one can ever rest satisfied that justice has been achieved.

Think of that demand for active justice in the face of the racial injustice that had plagued out country since its founding. In the 1860s, Americans believed that racism had ended with the victory over the Confederacy and the enactment of the thirteenth, fourteenth, and fifteenth Amendments. In the 1940s, many thought that racial justice had been achieved when the army was integrated. In the 1950s, we thought that justice had been achieved when the Supreme Court ordered desegregation of the public schools. In the 1960s, the civil rights and voting act promised equal justice. In every generation, the quest for justice has achieved better and better results. There is far more racial justice today than ever before in our history. But no one looking at today's America can rightfully conclude that we have achieved ultimate justice for African Americans. The same is true of other disadvantaged and discriminated-against groups. We are on a road that doesn't end.

We must never be content with the status quo, certainly as it regards justice. There is a line in *The Merchant of Venice* that implicitly makes this point. Shylock has been forced to convert on threat of death. When he is asked whether he has truly converted from Judaism to Christianity, he replies, "I am content." I have always thought that his answer proved beyond a doubt that he was no longer a Jew. Because no Jew is ever content. It is not in the nature of Jews to be content, and it is not in the nature of anyone who believes in the Bible to be content with the current state of justice.

The commentators on the Bible frequently ask why God repeated the words justice. Wouldn't it have been enough for Him to command, "Justice must you pursue?" But no: God says, "justice, justice." There are no extra words in the Bible. Every word has a meaning. So various commentaries have been offered in the meaning of the duplication. Some say that one reference is to substantive justice while the other is to procedural justice. Others say that one justice is for the victim, and the other for the accused. Still others say that there is no single definition of justice: we know injustice when we see it, but there is no agreement about what constitutes perfect justice. It is in the nature of Biblical commentary that it never ends. Every generation comes up with new interpretations and new insights as to the meanings of ancient words.

I was fortunate to have my Bar Mitzvah fall on the week in which this particular Biblical portion is read by Jews all around the world. I always believed that it sent me a message. I have devoted my life to seeking justice for others, from my earliest opposition to the death penalty while I was in high school, to the current pro bono work I do with Aleph, the wonderful Chabad organization that provides services to imprisoned men and women all over the world. Now, at age eighty-two, I am demanding justice for myself, against my false accuser. I have already achieved justice in terms of the evidence, which conclusively proves to any open-minded person that it is impossible that I would or could have done what she falsely accused me of. One would think that would be enough. But no, not in the age of cancel culture and #MeToo, where evidence and lack thereof counts for little.

What is most important in this age of identity politics is the identity of the accuser and the accused: always believe women, regardless of their history of lying, or regardless of the accused's history of truth-telling and sexual probity. The Bible teaches otherwise. In my portion, judges are directed not to take identity into account. The words in Hebrew are "*Lo takir panim*," which means do not base your decision on the faces or identities of the litigants. Base it instead on the facts and the evidence. I wish people today would abide by that 3000-year-old wisdom.

I also wish judges and prosecutors paid more heed to another command of my Bible portion: "The judges shall inquire diligently; and behold if the witness be a false witness and has testified falsely against his brother [or sister], then shall ye do unto him [or her] as he [or she] had proposed to do against unto his brother [or sister]." I have invited prosecutors and judges to "inquire diligently" into my accuser and me. If they do, they will conclude that she has "testified falsely" and should be punished under the law of perjury.

I, for one, will continue to live and work in the spirit of the commandment to chase after "justice, justice". Justice for those who have been sexually exploited. And justice for those who have been falsely accused—as Joseph in the Bible was—of sexual misconduct. I am confident that justice and truth will prevail in my case, no matter how long the road or how exhausting the chase.

I will also fight against the injustices of cancel culture, and especially its refusal to adhere to mandates of both the Bible and our Constitution.

CHAPTER 9

Cancelling Evidence, Science, and the Constitution: Arguments against Vaccines

———————

M any on the hard-left and hard-right share a common blindness toward science, evidence, and facts. Ideology trumps proof and determines truth. It is not surprising that, despite the scientific case for vaccines, there are anti-vaxxers on both extremes of the political spectrum.

I was recently being interviewed about current events when the subject suddenly turned to vaccination. I expressed a view I have held for half a century, namely, that it is constitutional for the government to compel citizens to be vaccinated against highly contagious deadly diseases. I did not think that was a controversial statement. Nor did I think it was controversial to say that I personally would be vaccinated if a safe vaccine were developed against COVID-19. I grew up during the polio epidemic, and our heroes were Jonas Salk and Albert Sabin, who developed the first vaccines that virtually eradicated the scourge of polio—a highly contagious illness that killed a close friend of mine in elementary school.

Nor am I alone in arguing that vaccination under such circumstances is constitutional. During the first decade of the twentieth century, the Supreme Court upheld mandatory vaccination against smallpox, a disease that had decimated the world for many years. I believe that the current Supreme Court—divided as it is in so many issues—would uphold a reasonable mandatory vaccination law. I was shocked, therefore, by the reaction to what I believed was a non-controversial statement. My emails included threats—both secular and religious—as well as anti-Semitic attacks. They also included some thoughtful criticism regarding my views and some material about the alleged dangers of some vaccines. Bobby Kennedy called and wrote me with some interesting information and offered to debate me on the issue—which I accepted.[1]

Let me be clear what my views are as a lifelong civil libertarian who is critical of excessive government powers. The government has no legitimate authority to compel a competent adult to accept medical treatment that benefits only him or her. For example, if a vaccine against cancer or heart disease were to be developed, we could each decide for ourselves whether to take it. I believe there is a right to die as well as to live. But if a vaccine is developed, tested, and designed to prevent the spread of COVID-19, smallpox, Ebola, polio, or other highly contagious deadly disease, and it is deemed safe by the authorized experts, the government has the power to compel you to take it—not for your own good, but for the good of those who might otherwise catch it from you and die. That has been my view for more than half a century. I put it this way many years ago in the context of cigarette smoking: "You have a right to inhale anywhere; but you have no right to exhale near me." This is a variation of the traditional civil-liberties mantra that "The right to swing your fist ends at the tip of my nose." Similarly, your "right" to have COVID-19 destroy your own lungs ends at the area around my nose, eyes, and mouth.

This means that the government can reasonably compel the wearing of masks, the requirement of social distancing, and the prevention of large gatherings. It can also compel vaccination to prevent you from transmitting a fatal disease to me.

Theoretically, you should have the option of opting out of the vaccine if you agree not to endanger me by remaining effectively quarantined during the duration of the pandemic. But this would be

---

1   The debate can be viewed on YouTube: https://www.youtube.com/watch?v=IfnJi7yLKgE.

difficult to enforce. It is also in the public good for everyone to be vaccinated in order to achieve maximum herd immunity.

In order to compel any potentially dangerous medical intrusion for the public good, the government should be required to assure maximum safety consistent with the imminent need for protection. There can never be an absolute guarantee of complete safety for any medical procedure, even an injection or pill. All that is constitutionally required in a democracy is a process for implementing the best judgment of highly qualified and objective experts and an ability to challenge legislation in the courts. That is true of all governmental actions that entail risks, ranging from military actions to fluoridating the water supply.

There will always be dissenters, and their right to oppose mandatory vaccinations and other governmental intrusions must be protected. The debates—medical, scientific, legal, moral, political—should go on. That is essential to the health of any democracy. But in the meantime, the government should act to protect us all from pandemics that endanger our lives.

I hope, therefore, that scientists around the world continue their important work toward developing an effective and safe vaccine to combat the current pandemic. That is the essential first step. Then comes the testing. But it is important to begin the discussion now about how to deal with those who will refuse to accept any vaccine, regardless of how safe and effective it may be.

Some of the objections are purportedly based on science, while others are rooted in religion. I addressed these objections in an op-ed shortly after New York eliminated religious objections to mandatory vacation.[2] My conclusion:

> "It was the right thing to do. There is no constitutional basis for requiring a religious exemption. Nor, in my view, are there any plausible religious arguments against mandatory vaccinations to spread communicable and potential lethal diseases."

---

2   Alan M. Dershowitz, "There Is No Religious Right to Refuse Vaccination", *New York Daily News*, June 14, 2019.

Let me justify my conclusion by first addressing any compelling religious arguments: _____.

I have left this blank because there are none. I read widely in religious literature, especially Jewish literature. I have never come across a coherent religious argument against mandatory vaccination for deadly contagious diseases. Jewish law has an overriding religious concept called *"pikuach nefesh,"*—the saving of lives—which elevates the protection of human life over nearly every other value.

The Jewish Bible is scrupulous in demanding protecting against communicable diseases such as leprosy. There is nothing in Jewish law that requires the parents to turn their children into "typhoid Marys," infecting friends, family, classmates, and neighbors.

The claimed religious argument is rejected by the vast majority of rabbis of every denomination, including by the vast majority of ultra-Orthodox and Hasidic rabbis. Only a handful of marginal rabbis preach this anti-Jewish and anti-life philosophy.

I challenge any rabbi to debate me on the Jewish religious law regarding vaccination and communicable diseases. He will lose the debate because there is simply no basis in Jewish law for any such argument. Religion is being used as a cover for a misguided political, ideological, conspiratorial, and personal opposition to vaccination. Don't believe any rabbi who tells you otherwise.

Let me now turn to the constitutional argument:

_____.

Another blank, because there is none that would permit a healthy adult to refuse to be vaccinated or parents to refuse to vaccinate a child against a communicable disease, even if there were plausible religious reasons for their decisions (which there are not).

There are three basic categories of compelled medical intervention about which the Constitution has something relevant to say.

The first category involves compelling a competent adult to take lifesaving measures to prevent his own death. There are strong constitutional and civil-liberties arguments against such compulsion. It really doesn't matter whether the opposition to such measures is religious or philosophical. An adult Jehovah's Witness may have a strong First Amendment claim against receiving a blood transfusion to save his or her life. But an atheist would also have a compelling argument. Indeed, Jewish law is more protective of life than American constitutional law: Jewish law prohibits a competent adult from refusing a lifesaving medical procedure. It also prohibits suicide.

The second category is where a parent is being compelled to employ lifesaving medical procedures to save the life of a child. The courts generally require the parent to save the life of a child. So a Jehovah's Witness child could be compelled to receive a blood transfer without regard to their parent's religious objection.

Now we get to the third category, the one about compelled measles or COVID-19 vaccination. A parent does not have a constitutional right to refuse to vaccinate a child against a highly contagious and potentially lethal disease which might kill that child (category two) but might also kill a friend or neighbor who doesn't share the parent's religious view (category three).

That is about the easiest constitutional question I have ever confronted. There is no compelling argument against requiring a child to be vaccinated against communicable diseases, regardless of the parents' wishes, and regardless of whether their objections are religious or secular.

Theoretically, a parent could move their case from category three to category two (or an adult could move it to category one) if there were an assurance that they would spend all their lives in a bubble that prevented contagious diseases from spreading. Or perhaps in a community of anti-vaxxers who would spread the disease only to other anti-vaxxers. The difference is between hurting oneself and hurting others.

The civil-libertarian position goes back to John Stuart Mill and even further in intellectual history. I can think of no thinker in history who has ever persuasively advocated the anti-vaccine position. There is no coherent argument—religious, constitutional, civil-libertarian or commonsensical—in favor of allowing people to refuse to be vaccinated against communicable diseases.

Beyond vaccine cancellation is the broader issue of science cancellation, which extends to climate-change denial, gun-violence denial, and other important policy issues.

Not that science is always right at every point in time. Throughout history, terrible things were done in the name of science: eugenic sterilization and euthanasia, "scientific" racism in Nazi Germany, as well as "scientific" anti-Semitism. But bad things have also been done in the name of religion, politics, and other ideologies. At the beginning of the COVID-19 pandemic, I wrote an article entitled: "Believe Science but be Skeptical of Scientists," which urged readers to be skeptical of experts who claim to have all the answers.

I am a skeptic by nature. I never believe what I read or hear without independently checking it. So when I read that public-health officials were urging people *not* to buy face masks, because they don't work, I was doubtful.

The officials also said that if individuals buy facemasks in large numbers, there won't be enough for health providers. That I believed. But the combination of reasons—they don't work, but they are important for health providers—immediately set off alarm bells in my skeptical mind.

If they don't work for ordinary individuals, why should they work for health providers?

Maybe there is a relevant difference. I kept an open but skeptical mind, while wearing the single N95 mask that I bought, just in case.

It now turns out that the public-health officials who were telling us not to buy masks were not telling us the whole truth. They were giving us only half the equation.

While it's true that a mass run on masks might deny them to health providers, it's equally true that masks may provide some layer of protection above and beyond the other precautions that everyone should take, such as handwashing and social distancing.

Those who misled us did so deliberately, but with a benign motive: they truly believed that it was more important for health providers to have masks than for every individual to stock up on them. When providers get sick, it has a greater impact on public health than if ordinary individuals catch the virus.

In order to make sure that individuals did not place their own safety above that of the community, a decision was made to present the facts in a skewed manner to disincentivize private purchases of masks.

Although well-intentioned, this deception backfired. Many people saw through the ruse and thought that what was good for health providers was good for them and their family, and they stocked up on masks. So we then had a situation where there was a run on masks, while at the same time there was a diminution in the credibility accorded those in charge of telling us how to react to the crisis.

The worst of both worlds. Honesty may not always be the best policy in extreme emergencies, but dishonesty—even when positively motivated—is not likely to work for long in a society in which social media amplifies the voices of critics, and reasonable people don't know who to believe.

Another claim about which I was skeptical was that the virus is only contagious by physical contact with infected individuals or surfaces that they touched.

Over and over again, it was emphasized that this particular virus could not be caught by airborne or aerosol transmission. In other words, it doesn't travel through the air. I was skeptical of this claim because it seemed inconsistent with the speed and frequency with which transmissions were occurring around the world.

I told my friends and family to act as if they could get the virus through the air. There is no downside to being more careful.

Subsequent research confirmed my skepticism. It now turns out that the virus can remain suspended in the air for a period of time, though it loses its potency while falling to the ground. This means that we are at risk of catching the virus even if we wear gloves, wash our hands, and avoid touching surfaces.

It probably also means that masks may be even more important than we were previously led to believe, even if we were skeptical about the "masks don't work at all" message.

These are only two examples of what are sure to be other false messages we have been receiving, especially in the early stages of the pandemic, when the science was more anecdotal than carefully researched. As more data emerges, we will receive more advice from scientists, most of which will probably be accurate, but some of which will almost certainly turn out to be less than fully accurate.

How should we assess this mélange of information, misinformation, partial truths, and outright falsehoods to which we are certain to be exposed? It won't be easy, especially in the age of social media, where everyone is an expert and all opinions are created "equally."

A cartoon that was recently circulated makes the point. It has a typical guy looking at his computer and saying: "That's odd: my Facebook friends who were constitutional scholars just a month ago are now infectious disease experts. . . ."

In a democracy permeated by social media, everyone becomes an expert on everything at the click of a computer. This is not an argument against science. It is an argument in favor of carefully assessing, evaluating, comparing, and challenging scientific claims. But in the end, the best policies must be based on the best science. If we cancel science, we cancel truth.

It is also an argument against not exploiting or distorting science or events that give rise to the need for science in order to obtain ideological or partisan advantage.

As the coronavirus ravages the world, partisans on both sides seek to exploit it to their advantage. Opponents of choice are trying to shut down abortion clinics as "non-essential" medical facilities. Second Amendment zealots are seeking to reduce checks on gun possession. Environmental extremists are suggesting permanent restrictions on the use of airplanes and other means of travel that cause pollution. Advocates of universal healthcare are demanding it now, despite its failure to prevent the spread of the pandemic in countries that have it. Both parties, but especially the Republicans, are seeking voting rules that will help them at the polls. But most perverse is the new campaign to end the so-called pandemic of pornography, which has apparently spread now that so many people are home alone with only their computers.

Anti-porn zealots offer the following comparison between the coronavirus and pornography:

> Like the coronavirus, pornography use is silent but deadly, a powerful disease that has had devastating effects across our society. Although coronavirus may attract more headlines today,

pornography will be with us for the long haul. Porn cannot be vaccinated against. It has a nearly $100 billion industry devoted to its
spread worldwide and few are brave enough to stand against it.

Any analogy between a pandemic that threatens the lives of millions
of innocent men, women, and children, and the voluntary use of
pornography by adults is, of course, absurd. Anti-porn zealots claim,
however, that the use of porn is not voluntary—that it is addictive,
just like crack cocaine and heroin. They warn about "addictions to
greater amounts and more depraved forms of porn." Although there
is no scientific basis for this claim, it is commonly made by those who
would make pornography illegal.

Anti-porn zealots are now focusing on porn sites that usually
charge for access, but are now making it free, in order to encourage
people to stay home and watch it rather than risk sex with potentially infected partners. Then they point to the following new phenomenon: "Perhaps most disturbingly, Vice News reported earlier
this month on a surge of coronavirus-themes on porn sites such as
Pornhub and xHamster, proving a well-known internet maxim that
"There is nothing—absolutely nothing—pornography won't sexual-
ize if it won't make them a profit." Apparently these sites show porn
actors and actresses wearing protective masks. How that poses any
danger, the critics don't explain.

They do, however, declare "The explosion of online pornography
to be a public health crisis, recognizing the serious threat it poses to
use all." They claim that this is "no exaggeration." But surely it is.

I have no problem with anti-porn crusaders exercising their First
Amendment rights in an effort to try and deny First Amendment
rights to producers and consumers of adult pornography. The marketplace of ideas should be open to all, even during times of crisis. We
are already experiencing diminutions in our constitutional rights to
assemble, to travel, to go to church, to work, and to gather with family.
But these emergency measures are temporary and deemed necessary
by public-health officials. What the anti-porn zealots are trying to do
is, in their own words, *permanently* stifle the free expression of sexual
images they deem offensive. They are using the current pandemic as

an excuse to get what they have been trying to get for years. But they picked the wrong time, because if there ever was a justification for "home remedies" to sexual deprivation, this may be that time.

An op-ed by the Executive Director of the American Principles Project insists that: "As bad as coronavirus is, we cannot afford to fight one disease by simply trading it for another. Now more than ever, we must join together to take on the pornography industry and defeat the terrible porn epidemic."

I would respond by saying, now more than ever, we must not devote additional resources to unnecessarily constraining basic liberties that are unrelated to the public-health need to prevent the spread of the coronavirus.

Moving to a more serious issue, some states, especially Texas, have been trying to shut down abortion clinics, claiming they provide non-essential medical procedures. But as the CEO of the Center for Reproductive Rights correctly pointed out, "It is very clear that anti-abortion rights politicians are shamelessly exploiting this crisis to achieve what has been their longstanding ideological goal to ban abortion in the United States." To prove that point, she cites efforts by some states to ban abortion pills, as well as other methods of ending pregnancy that do not require hospitalization or clinics. She also points out that banning abortion is far more dangerous to public health because it will force women to travel long distances. They site a study that women seeking abortions during this pandemic would have to travel up to twenty times further than normal if some states shut down local clinics.

Some radical feminists may be conflicted over these issues: they support choice when it comes to abortion, but reject choice when it comes to pornography. Consistency may not be required in making private choices, but it is important with regard to public policy.

Another area of potential conflict between science and the Constitution arises when scientists urge citizens not to exercise their constitutional rights to protest, pray, or assemble.

The right to protest is guaranteed by our First Amendment. So is the right to assemble peaceably and petition the government. And so is the right to pray in a house of prayer. But officials have the power to impose time-and-manner restrictions on these important rights. No one has the right to play their loudspeakers and wake up neighbors in the middle of the night, or to break into legislative assemblies to present their petitions, or to assemble on private property without any permission from the owner, or to block the entrance to a public building.

Against this background, the question arises whether the citizens who are protesting current restrictions on movement have the constitutional right to assemble in violation of social-distancing rules. They certainly have the right to petition across social media and in other ways that do not endanger public health. But do they have the constitutional right to gather together with large crowds to express their views? The answer depends on several factors.

The first is whether the social-distancing rules are legally enforceable. The president and governors generally have no authority to make laws, since only legislatures may make laws that are enforceable through arrest and prosecution. Under certain circumstances, legislatures may delegate the authority to make enforceable rules to the executive branch, meaning the president, governors, or mayors, but that should be express and specific. Executives have no inherent power to create restrictions on liberty absent this, and they generally enforce laws enacted by legislatures. The President of the United States is *not* the commander-in-chief of our *citizens*; he is only the commander-in-chief of our armed forces. Soldiers must follow his orders, but civilians need not, unless they are authorized by law.

Some of the state executive orders restricting liberty are of questionable validity absent legislative authorization. That does not mean they should not be obeyed, but it does mean that if they are not obeyed, it could be difficult to enforce them through criminal punishment. If the shutdowns do remain in place for a considerable period of time, legislation may be required to authorize such long-term restrictions on freedom.

So the question surrounding the recent protests in Washington, Oregon, Wisconsin, Michigan, Virginia, and elsewhere is whether the protesters were actually violating any enforceable criminal laws or merely disregarding any unenforceable executive orders. That is usually a question of local law that needs to be answered before we get to rights under the First Amendment.

Only if the rules banning protesters gathering are legally enforceable under state law do we then reach the question of whether these rules violate the First Amendment. That may depend on how broad the rules are. If they are narrowly tailored to the current crisis, they will probably pass muster under the First Amendment. But if they are vague and not limited in time, they may be found to violate the Constitution.

As Supreme Court Justice Robert Jackson has said, "the Constitution is not a suicide pact." It must be flexible enough to assure that, during real emergencies, the government must have the authority, as Thomas Jefferson noted, "of self-preservation and of saving our country when in danger." However, the Constitution must also serve as a barrier against governments exploiting crises to expand their powers beyond the real needs of the moment. That is happening in Hungary, Turkey, and other authoritarian regimes around the world. It must not be allowed to happen in this country.

The judiciary, especially the Supreme Court, comprise the government institutions that have been authorized to strike this delicate balance. In general, the judiciary has struck it in favor of emergency powers used during real public health crises, so long as these executive powers are narrowly drawn, reasonably exercised, and limited in time.

Consider the closing of churches. It may be reasonable to prevent large crowds from gathering in closed buildings to worship, but it may not be reasonable to prevent people from sitting in their cars and listening to a sermon at an outdoor theater that has been converted into a temporary church. Or consider the people driving their cars in front of government buildings and honking their horns during the day in protest or flying flags upside down. Such accommodations may indeed be required by the First Amendment, even during real public-health emergencies, if these actions do not pose reasonable threats of spreading the coronavirus.

It may also violate the First Amendment to discriminate against houses of prayer when secular institutions that pose comparable public health threats are allowed to remain open.

Setting aside all the legal and constitutional issues, good citizens should comply with reasonable measures designed by responsible officials to prevent or control the spread of this highly contagious and deadly illness. Just because there is a right to protest does not necessarily mean it is fine to fully exercise that right, when to do so may endanger your family, your neighbors, or your community. A case in point is that protesters may have the right to yell at and insult health workers, but to do so is wrong. Do the right thing, even if you have the right to do the wrong thing.

In the end, science always prevails. It cannot be permanently cancelled, because it is based on what the world actually is, not what some want it to be. We can constrain science and limit its destructive capabilities, while encouraging its constructive contributions.

Science is a process for reaching certain testable truths. There may be other truths as well—religious, moral, ideological, political—which are not testable by empirical methods. But even these "truths" will not long endure if they conflict with science.

CHAPTER 10

Cancelling Elections

The most frightening use of the world "cancel" in recent months has been the threat of cancelling or postponing elections, especially the presidential election.

Tyrannical regimes use this tactic to remain in power. Even democratic regimes, such as New Zealand, have postponed elections because of the pandemic.

What if the pandemic were to get so bad in the United States that the election could not be held? There is no acceptable reason for this to happen, since there are alternatives to live voting on a single day. But it is possible, though unlikely, that voting by mail might become unrealistic if the pandemic were to become so much worse that it endangered the lives of postal workers.

So it is not too early to ask the question: What does the Constitution provide in the event that an emergency precludes an election before the end of the president's term? It has never happened before, and it probably won't happen this year, but law professors specialize in assessing hypothetical scenarios, so here is my assessment.

We begin, of course, with the words of the Constitution which, however, provide no definitive answer. But they do provide some clear conclusions. Absent an election, the incumbent president does not continue to serve in an interim capacity until an election is finally held. Unlike some other countries where an incumbent serves until replaced, the term of our president ends on a specific date, regardless of whether or not a successor has been picked.

The twentieth Amendment specifies that: "The terms of the president and vice president shall end at noon" on the twentieth of January. Nothing could seem clearer. Yet then, the end of that paragraph provides that "the terms of their successors shall then begin." But what if no successors have been elected? Does the president then continue to serve as an interim office holder? The answer is no, because his or her "term" definitely ends at noon on the twentieth of January. If not re-elected, he becomes a private citizen on that day. Who then serves as President? The Constitution itself provides no clear answer.

Unlike when a president is impeached or dies, there is no clear succession plan in place for a situation in which there has been no voting. Nor does the Twelfth Amendment provide guidance if there is no election. It provides for the House of Representatives to choose the president if no candidate receives a majority of the electoral vote in an election.

The twentieth Amendment does speak to the issue of what happens if neither a president nor a vice president shall have been chosen "before the time fixed for the beginning of his term," but it refers to a somewhat different scenario:

> "Congress may by law provide for the case wherein neither a President elect nor a Vice President elect shall have qualified, declaring who shall then act as President, or the manner in which one who is to act shall be selected, and such person shall act accordingly until a President or Vice president shall have qualified." (Emphasis added)

But if there is no election, there is no President or Vice President elect. Congress has provided for a line of succession "If by reason of death, resignation, removal from office, inability or failure to qualify," there is "Neither a President nor Vice President." Again, this does not seem to encompass the absence of an election. There is an obvious gap in our constitution, because the framers didn't contemplate a no- election possibility. But even if Congress has the authority to fill the constitutional gap, it isn't clear they have so with the current succession law, because the line of succession begins with the Speaker of the House.

But there would be no Speaker if there were no national elections, because there would be no House, all of whose members would be up for election in November. The terms of all members of the House would end, according to the Constitution, on the third of January. There would be a Senate, with two-thirds of its members who were not up for election still serving.

This is important, because the next in line for the presidency would be the president pro tempore of the Senate, who is currently Republican senator Charles Grassley. But if there were no election, there might be a Democratic majority among the remaining two-thirds of the senators who were not up for re-election. (Unless governors or state legislatures were allowed to fill vacant Senate seats—another uncertainty.) Traditionally, the longest-serving majority senator is given the honor of serving as president pro tem. Currently, that would be Democratic Senator Patrick Leahy of Vermont. But the Democratic majority could elect any sitting senator to that role, even Bernie Sanders. If the succession statute covers a non-election, which itself is doubtful, the Democratic senator selected to serve as president pro tem would become the next President.

The alternatives to an election are unthinkable in a democracy: a nation with no president and working legislature, or an interim president not clearly authorized by law.

Because of the utter uncertainty of any alternative to an election, it is in the interest of both parties and all Americans to make sure that the 2020 election is held in a timely, fair and safe manner.

So it is extremely unlikely that a presidential election could ever be cancelled, but it is highly likely that the results of such an election may be hotly disputed, as they were in 2000.

CHAPTER 11

Could a President Cancel Due Process by Declaring Martial Law?

The ultimate cancellation of constitutional rights, especially due process, would occur if a president tried to declare martial law in response to a national crisis, such as an even-worse pandemic, or an increase in violence growing out of demonstrations against racial injustice, or a disputed election that resulted in violence.

The Constitution, quite surprisingly, is silent on the issue of martial law. This is surprising because martial law was not uncommon at the founding, and several state constitutions provided for it in cases of emergency. The closest the Constitution comes is in declaring a prohibition against suspending the writ of habeas corpus "unless when in cases of rebellion or invasion the public safety may require it." We are definitely not experiencing an invasion; nor do the current disturbances—violent as some (but not others) have been—qualify as a rebellion. Accordingly, even if the president were to try to declare martial law, claiming that it is inherent in his power as commander-in-chief of the armed forces, the courts would have the last word, because citizens detained without due process would be able to secure judicial review by means of the "great writ" of *habeas corpus*.

What then would the courts do if the president were to declare martial law and have the military detain protesters? The answer is crystal clear: no one knows. There are no direct precedents for such an action when our nation is not at war. Even the wartime precedents speak with different voices. President Lincoln suspended *habeas corpus* during the rebellion we call the Civil War. President Roosevelt ordered the confinement of more than 100,000 Americans of Japanese descent after Pearl Harbor, and martial law was declared in the then territory of Hawaii. In a case growing out of the civil war, the justices used soaring language, pointing out that the framers:

> [F]oresaw that troublous times would arise, when rulers and people would become restrive under restraint, and seek by sharp and decisive measures to accomplish ends deemed just and proper; and that the principles of constitutional liberty would be in peril, unless established by irreparable law . . .
>
> The nation . . . has no right to expect that it will always have wise and humane rulers, sincerely attached to the principles of the Constitution. Wicked men, ambitious of power with hatred of liberty and contempt of law, may fill the place once occupied by Washington and Lincoln, and if this right [to suspend the provisions of the Constitution during the great exigencies of government] is conceded, and the calamities of war again befall us, the dangers to human liberty are frightful to contemplate.

But despite this language, the court allowed the detention of the citizen.

Governors have declared martial law in response to all manner of domestic disturbances, ranging from strikes, to riots, to disputes over oil production. In a case involving a conflict between coal miners and owners, Justice Oliver Wendell Holmes, Jr. wrote that a governor may seize "the bodies of those whom he considers to stand in the way of restoring peace." The courts have generally not intruded on the exercise of such extraordinary powers while the emergencies persisted, but have insisted that they end when the emergency is over.

The history of martial law in our states has been decidedly mixed, with numerous abuses and excesses. This should not be surprising, since "martial law" is a contradiction in terms. If it's martial—that is, the rule of the military or the police—it isn't law. It's power.

If a president, as distinguished from a governor, decided to declare martial law throughout the entire nation, or even in selected states or regions, would he need the approval of Congress? A related question is whether Congress has already given the president the authority to declare martial law or suspend individual rights.

There are several statutes that may be relevant, but none that are definitive. Were the president to claim that the combination of violent disruptions and the threat of a renewed spread of the coronavirus justified the use of the military and/or the suspension of certain basic rights, he would be embarking on uncharted waters. So would the courts. There is no governing precedent for a combination of dangers such as the ones we face today. The courts would look to past invocations of martial law and emergency powers for guidance.

In a recent op-ed, *New York Times* journalist Linda Greenhouse reported on the existence of presidential emergency-action documents that lie "deep under the radar, ready to be invoked without Congressional oversight or even notice":

> The text of these documents, numbering between 50 and 60 . . . has never been released, and the powers the documents purport to grant the president have evidently never been invoked. They are thought to authorize such drastic actions as the presidential suspension of habeas corpus, warrantless searches and the imposition of martial law.

Back in the early 1970s, I wrote a series of articles about the history of martial law and emergency powers. This is how I summarized our mixed record:

> What then could we reasonably expect from our courts if any American president during a period of dire emergency were once again to suspend important constitutional safeguards? Our past experiences suggest the following outline: The courts—especially the Supreme Court—will generally not interfere with the

executive's handling of a genuine emergency while it still exists. They will employ every technique of judicial avoidance at their disposal to postpone decision until the crisis has passed. (Indeed, though thousands of persons have been unlawfully confined during our various periods of declared emergency, I am aware of no case where the Supreme court has ever actually ordered anyone's release while the emergency was still in existence.) The likely exceptions to this rule of judicial postponement will be cases of clear abuse where no real emergency can be said to exist, and cases in which delay would result in irrevocable loss of rights, such as those involving the death penalty. Once the emergency has passed, the courts will generally not approve further punishment; they will order the release of all those sentenced to imprisonment or death in violation of ordinary constitutional safeguards. But they will not entertain damage suits for illegal confinement ordered during the course of the emergency.

Let us hope that we never get to a point where martial law or other emergency measures that curtail fundamental rights are deemed necessary. If we do, there are no absolute guarantees in our Constitution or in our precedents to assure that the proper balance will be struck. The Constitution must never be cancelled. Its provisions were designed to be adaptive to any crises our nation may face. Like democracy itself, our living constitution is not perfect, just better, more enduring, and more tested than other parchment protections throughout the ages.

CHAPTER 12

What It Feels Like to Be Falsely Cancelled

I was looking forward to New Year's of 2015. I had taught at Harvard Law School for fifty years. Though I was controversial because of my iconoclastic views and my "Dickensonian" mix of guilty and innocent clients (as one journalist put it), my personal life was without blemish. In my half-century at Harvard, teaching thousands of women and employing dozens of female research and secretarial assistants, not a single complaint had ever been made against me.

I had recently retired after turning seventy-five, and I was being honored by universities, Jewish organizations, and other institutions, for my lifelong commitment to civil liberties, human rights, the rule of law, and Israel. Presidents Clinton and Obama wrote in praise of my accomplishments. They were joined by others, including Israeli prime ministers and justices. I was the most sought-after speaker for Jewish groups and one of the most sought-after by other groups. I was on top of the world, expecting the remainder of my life to be easy and filled with the joy of doing exactly what I wanted to do while my wife and I enjoyed our families and friends.

Little did I know that a small group of people were planning to cancel my life in order to enrich themselves. They conspired to "pressure" a woman I never met to accuse me of something I never did. They knew they were making up the entire story, but they didn't care, because they planned to publicize the maliciously false accusation against me to extort a billion dollars from the multi-billionaire owner of The Limited and Victoria's Secret, Leslie Wexner. The plan was simple: make the accusation against me public and then privately approach Wexner and demand a billion dollars in hush money.

And so, on the day before New Year's eve, they filed the false accusation against me and leaked it to the media. At the same time, they privately and secretly accused Wexner of nearly identical misconduct. The message to Wexner was clear: we will do to you what we did to Dershowitz unless you pay us megabucks. I was never supposed to find out about the Wexner shakedown, and probably never would have if the childhood best friend of my false accuser had not called to tell me that my accuser had told her the accusation against me was false and that she was pressured to make it up as part of a plan to obtain a billion dollars from Wexner. The best friend didn't want to hurt my accuser, but she felt terrible about me being falsely accused, so she called me. My false accuser was furious with her friend for disclosing the truth.

I have described elsewhere, in my book *Guilt by Accusation*, and in parts of this book, the incontrovertible evidence, in my accuser's own words and those of lawyers and friends, that prove I never met her. The purpose of this chapter is not to rehearse that evidence. Its purpose is to describe what can happen to a completely innocent person who is victimized by false accusers in a world in which the media is all too anxious to promote wild and uncorroborated accusations, because false accusations are more salacious and better for sales and awards than truthful denials. This is especially so if the accused person is well-known and controversial. As my mother cautioned me when I began to appear in the public eye: "The higher you go, the longer the fall." But there is a significant difference between falling on one's own and being pushed off a cliff by mendacious criminals.

Nor is it the purpose of this chapter to make the reader feel sorry for me. I am not looking for sympathy. I'm looking to make sure that what has happened to me does not happen to other innocent people.

If this can happen to me, it can happen to your father, grandfather, son, brother, or sister. I want the reader to understand the impact a false accusation could have on someone who has lived a good and honorable life for three-quarters of a century and is suddenly accused of something he would never do. I want them to know how it feels to be falsely accused and cancelled.

For purposes of reading this chapter, the readers should assume—as the evidence proves—that I am telling the truth: that the accusations against are totally made up and I am entirely innocent. It is from that premise that I will describe the impact the false accusations have had on me and my family. I want every reader to imagine what it would feel like if your life's work—or that of someone close to you—was being cancelled because of an entirely false accusation that many believe is true, despite conclusive evidence that I never even met my accuser. It may be difficult for someone who has never been falsely accused to imagine what it feels like. I know that despite having represented falsely accused defendants, I had no real appreciation of the impact on an innocent person until it happened to me. I could not even imagine what it would feel like to have one's entire history of good deeds cancelled by a made-up story. I am now far more motivated than ever to help vindicate other falsely accused innocents. I am more motivated to help assure that those who falsely accuse innocent people are held accountable. It is difficult to imagine how a false accuser must feel, knowing that she has destroyed the life of an innocent person, and that she has hurt the cause of real victims of abuse by her lies. She would have to have no conscience, no sense of right and wrong, to victimize innocent people in this way.

I am eighty-two years old, happily married for thirty-four years, with three children and two grandchildren. I do not flirt, hug, touch, or do anything even arguably inappropriate sexually. My grandchildren and daughter are part of the young generation that includes many supporters of cancel culture and #MeToo. Although none of my family members or friends believe I did anything wrong—indeed, no objective person who knows me or who has read what I have written believes that—many people associated with them either believe it or suspect it may be true. My family members, too, have suffered from the false accusation. It is devastating to me to know that people actually believe an accusation that has been disproved by such overwhelming evidence, but that is the reality of today's world. If you don't think that it is true, go on Twitter or other social media. The damage to me is pervasive. It impacts every aspect of my personal and professional life. People look at me differently. They interact with me differently. It has changed my life, despite the proved reality that I have done nothing wrong. I am the victim of a serious crime, yet I am treated as a perpetrator. Talk about "blaming the victim!"

As far as cancel culture is concerned, I have only been a partial victim. As a result of this false accusation, I have been cancelled as a speaker at universities, for fear of protests.[1] I have been cancelled by many speaking venues, including, as I previously mentioned, the 92nd Street Y. I will never again get an honorary degree from any university, having received more than a dozen preceding the false accusation. The plans to fund a chair professorship in my name have been put on hold. Proposals to honor me with awards for my work have been cancelled. My reputation and legacy have been damaged.

Although I have the best winning record of any appellate defense lawyer in capital and homicide cases (approximately eighty-five percent), I am sure that some potential clients have decided to go to other lawyers for fear of being prejudiced by the false accusation against me. I have been cancelled by several media outlets—newspapers, TV, magazines. My biography, and, as I previously mentioned, my obit, will highlight the false accusation, accompanied by my denial, but without cataloging the overwhelming evidence of my innocence.

I still write op-eds, speak in some venues, and consult on cases all around the world. I am not a victim of total cancellation, as some have been. But then again, although I have only been partially cancelled, I am not partially guilty. I am totally innocent. I did absolutely nothing wrong. Yes, I was Jeffrey Epstein's lawyer, and helped

---

1   On September 15th, 2020, students at Yale Law School, from which I graduated with honors, protested an invitation to me to discuss the constitutional criteria for impeachment with Professor Akhil Amar.

get him what many regard as a favorable plea bargain, but that is my job as a criminal defense lawyer. From the day I met Epstein until today, I have never had sexual contact with any woman other than my wife. I have never had sexual contact with any underage person. But because there is no current forum in which to prove my innocence by presenting the evidence, the presumption of guilt hangs over me. I am suing my accuser and her lawyer, and will be able to prove my innocence when the case come to trial. But the trial is a long way off, especially in light of the pandemic. I only hope I will live and remain healthy long enough to present the incontrovertible case for my innocence as only I can do.

I am strong, resilient, and have the resources necessary to fight back against these false accusations. I will not rest until no rational person can possible believe that I did anything wrong. But in the meantime—and most of life is lived in the "meantime"—I will have to live with my long history of doing good being at least partially cancelled. I am now widely known as the guy who had sex with the Epstein "girl," rather than the professor who taught 10,000 students, saved innocent lives, defended Israel against bigoted accusations, helped raise a wonderful family, and lived a life of personal and professional probity. All because a woman with a long history of making up false stories about famous people for money decided to conspire with lawyers of questionable ethics to falsely accuse me of a sin they know I did not commit. That is the unfairness of cancel culture.

Conclusion

Cancel culture is a cancer on American democracy, meritocracy, due process, and freedom of expression. It is metastasizing through social media. It is chilling creativity, endangering basic liberties, miseducating students, erasing history, empowering extremists, destroying hard-earned legacies—all without accountability or transparency. Cancel culture is real. It is a not an exaggeration concocted by right-wing extremists to discredit the left, the woke, or progressives. It is having a significant impact not only on the people who have themselves been cancelled, but on the many more who have been denied the music, the art, the teaching, the advocacy, and other benefits previously bestowed by those who have been cancelled. Recently, some woke music critics have been trying to cancel Beethoven,[1] calling his music the "soundtrack" for "white privilege" and oppression.

Has cancel culture done any good by focusing attention on people who may have done bad things or promoted bad values? Actually, no! There are better ways to confront the evils of the past, with scalpels, not sledgehammers, bulldozers, and erasers. History should

---

1   Jonathan Tobin, "Cancelling Beethoven Is the Latest Woke Madness for the Classical-Music World", *New York Post*, September 17, 2020.

be continuously revised based on new information and changing values. The law provides remedies for current and recent wrongdoing. The media has the capacity to report in a nuanced and calibrated way. Individuals have the right to pass personal judgment on those with whom they interact, and on those who seek their vote or business. Public protests against those who do wrong are protected by our Constitution. Other institutions—universities, businesses, government agencies—have mechanisms in place to process complaints. But every process must provide for a reasonable opportunity to respond and correct errors.

Cancel culture causes more problems than it solves. It falsely accuses; it applies a double standard of selectivity; it fails to balance or calibrate vices and virtues; it has no statute of limitations; it provides no process to challenge cancellations; it is standardless, unaccountable, not transparent, and often anonymous; it hides personal, ideological, and political agendas; it can be abused for revenge, extortion, and other malign motives; it is un-American to the core. It must be stopped, lest it destroy the heart, soul, and values of our nation.

It won't be easy to cancel cancel culture, because, like all "cultures," it is diffuse; it has no home-office or headquarters; no one is in charge; the buck stops nowhere. Cancel culture must be contested in the marketplace of ideas. Those of us who love liberty, defend due process, support free speech, favor meritocracy, despise bullies, oppose identity politics, demand equality for all, value the search for truth, and reject political correctness must fight back against the great "dangers to liberty [that] lurk in the insidious encroachment by men [and women] of zeal, well meaning, but without understandings." We must cancel cancel culture now, before it becomes the American culture.

Appendix I: Partial List of Individuals Who Have Recently Been Cancelled or Have Had Speeches or Appearances Cancelled

Acosta, Alex. Former United States Attorney for the Southern District of Florida and former United States Labor Secretary was forced to resign as Labor Secretary after being criticized for the deal he made with Jeffrey Epstein.

Adams, Ryan. According to CNN, Ryan exchanged a few thousand-text messages with an underage girl. He never met the girl and claims he thought she was older, but many doubt this story. In some of the texts he would remind her she could not tell her mother they were texting. This resulted in canceled tours in the UK and the US.

Adams, Sam. Director of the United States Branch of the World Resources Institute accused of sexual harassment. Resigned but claims the decision was unrelated to the accusations.

Alexander, Joe. Chief Creative Officer of the Martin Agency accused of sexual harassment by multiple employees. Resigned.

Allen, Woody. Accused of molesting his adopted daughter when she was a child. Most recently, Hachette Book Group, announced it would not be publishing Allen's memoir *Apropos of Nothing*. Hachette made the decision after receiving backlash from outsiders and from staff members. Skyhorse ultimately published it. Amazon also canceled his most recent film, but later showed it on TV.

Arce, Angel. Connecticut State Representative accused of sending inappropriate messages to a teenage girl. Resigned.

Ashbrook, Tom. Host of WBUR's *On Point* accused of bullying, unwanted touching and sexual misconduct (multiple employees). According to *The New York Times*, an investigation found the behavior was "not sexual in nature."

Ayers, H. Brandt. Chairman of Consolidated Publishing accused of sexual assault. Resigned.

Barr, Roseanne. Barr had a history of offensive tweets but one was particularly racially insensitive. According to *The Hollywood Reporter*, Barr tweeted about former President Barack Obama's senior advisor, Valerie Jarrett, "Muslim brotherhood & planet of the apes had a baby=vj." ABC canceled the *Roseanne* show.

Becerra, Xavier. According to thefire.org—an organization committed to protecting the fundamental rights of students on college campuses—in 2017, California Attorney General Xavier Becerra, was essentially denied the ability to answer audience questions at Whittier College by Trump supporters wearing MAGA hats. They were there in protest of the Attorney General's lawsuit against the decision to rescind DACA. The event was forced to end early. FIRE attributed the cause to "Substantial Event Disruption" and notes: "The event was forced to conclude early when the hecklers would not cease interrupting."

Bennett, James. Former Editorial Page Editor of *The New York Times*. Bennett resigned after publishing a highly criticized opinion piece.

Berganza, Eddie. According to *The New York Times*, the editor at DC Comics, "forcibly kissed and tried to grope colleagues." Fired.

Besh, John. Chief Executive of the Besh Restaurant Group accused of sexual harassment (multiple people). Resigned.

Bittel, Stephen. Chairman of the Florida Democratic Party accused of sexually inappropriate comments and behavior. Resigned.

Bocanegra, Raul. California State Assemblyman accused of sexual harassment (multiple women). Resigned.

Bomberger, Ryan. The President of Radiance Foundation (pro-life advocacy group) was scheduled to speak at UT Austin. Protesters ignited a smoke bomb causing the alarm to go off and the event was disrupted and moved to another location.

Boyens, Max. The cast member on *Vanderpump Rules* posted racist tweets and was fired from the show (along with fellow cast member Brett Caprioni).

Braun, Kevin. The Editor in Chief of E&E News was accused of sexual harassment by multiple staff members. Soon thereafter, Braun left his role in management but is still co-owner of E&E.

Burwell, Robert. Queens University renamed its administration building from Burwell Hall to Queens Hall. The Reverend Robert Burwell and his wife were said to own and abuse slaves.

Cannon, Nick. Cannon made anti-Semitic comments during a "Cannon's Class" podcast and ViacomCBS fired him as host of *Wild n' Out*.

Calhoun, John C. Yale renamed Calhoun College. Clemson University renamed its honors college, which was named after the former United States Vice President and Senator. According to sc.edu, Calhoun was a slaveholder as well as "an ardent defender of slavery" and "chief architect of the political system that allowed slavery to exist." A Clemson University biography claims Calhoun was "an ardent believer in white supremacy." In Charleston, S.C., a resolution was recently approved to remove a statue of Calhoun.

Capó Crucet, Jennine. The author was canceled as a guest speaker at Georgia Southern University. Students protested Capó Crucet's appearance to discuss diversity on campus. According to thefire. org, some were upset that her book, "Make Your Home Among Strangers: A Novel," portrays "racism towards white people." Following the Q & A, approximately 20 - 30 students burned copies of her book and it was reported a group of protesters gathered outside her hotel causing her to switch locations. Her 2nd day appearance was canceled.

Caprioni, Brett. The cast member on *Vanderpump Rules* posted racist tweets and was fired from the show (along with fellow cast member Max Boyens).

Carlbach, Shlomo. A loving and affectionate man - accused posthumously of inappropriate touching by several women. Although Carlebach could not defend himself, several venues canceled his music.

Carmack, Edward. A statue of the former US Senator, who had a reputation of attacking civil rights advocates, was toppled in Nashville, Tennessee.

Charles, James. The beauty and make-up YouTube sensation lost 3 million subscribers (including Miley Cyrus and Kylie Jenner who stopped following him on Instagram) after a former mentor, who owns a vitamin company, publicly called Charles out for posting an ad by a rival supplement company.

C.K., Louis. Admitted to sexual misconduct (multiple women). This resulted in a lost production deal with FX, a cancelled film he wrote and starred in, and his role in *The Secret Life of Pets*.

Coleman, Corey J. According to *The New York Times*, an internal investigation found "deeply disturbing" sexual misconduct from the head of human resources for FEMA. Resigned.

Columbus, Christopher. Statues of Columbus were removed from several U.S. cities this year: New York, Boston, Richmond, Chicago and St. Paul.

Copley, John. According to *The New York Times*, the stage director for the Metropolitan Opera was accused "of making a sexually charged remark to a member of the chorus." Fired.

Cops. Following the George Floyd protests, the TV show known for glorifying police officers was canceled after 33 seasons.

Cornish, Tony. Minnesota State Representative accused of propositioning lawmakers/lobbyists for sex. Resigned.

Cosby, Bill. The actor was accused of drugging and raping multiple women. Cosby received a prison sentence and lost out on multiple deals, including *Bill Cosby 77*, a Netflix stand-up comedy special.

Coulter, Ann. In November of 2019, Coulter—a conservative political commentator known for her anti-immigrant stance—was met by hundreds of protestors at UC Berkeley for a scheduled appearance. Coulter was invited by the Berkeley College Republicans to speak on the subject of immigration, titled "Adios, America." *The Guardian* reported that over one thousand protestors attempted to block attendees from entering the event by linking their arms.

They shouted, "Go home Nazis!" and "Shame!" According to *USA Today*, attendees were escorted in and out of the event by police officers. Coulter was also scheduled to appear at UC Berkeley but that event was cancelled and a suit was filed against the university for "discriminating against conservative speakers." Chancellor Nicholas Dirks released a statement denying Berkeley cancelled the event, but admitting to imposing security restrictions on the time and location of the speech. *The New York Times* reported Coulter pulled out of the event as a result of losing the support of several conservative groups sponsoring her appearance in addition to Berkeley changing the date and time of her appearance, "when there were likely to be fewer students on campus and less of a likelihood for violent outbreaks." *The Guardian* reported Berkeley spent approximately $800,000 for security on the event that was ultimately cancelled.

Dababneh, Matt. California State Assemblyman accused of sexual harassment and masturbating in front of one of his accusers. Resigned.

Davis, Jefferson. A statue of Davis in Richmond, Virginia was recently toppled over by protestors. According to battlefields.org, the Confederate President who fled from Richmond as the Union Army advanced "believed in the importance of the institution of slavery for the south."

Dershowitz, Alan. I was invited by the Alaska Bar Association to be the keynote speaker at its annual event. Soon after the announcement was made, the Bar received complaints from some of its members. In particular, Scott Kendall, an Anchorage attorney took issue with the fact that Alaska reports some of the highest sexual assault crimes against women in the nation and I represented many clients who have been accused of such crimes—most recently Jeffrey Epstein as well as Mike Tyson and O.J. Simpson. I have also represented women who have been abused. I was being canceled for doing my job. As a result of the complaints, the board scheduled a special meeting to determine whether the offer would be rescinded. Before they had a chance to meet, the Bar cancelled the event due to Covid-19 as well as other unspecified reasons. I was also canceled by the 92nd Street Y.

Dick, Andy. The actor was accused of sexual harassment. Fired from two films.

Domingo, Placido. The renowned opera singer was accused by numerous women of sexual harassment. American theater companies canceled performances while most European counterparts continued to support him.

Dominguez, Jorge I. Professor at Harvard University and Chair of the Harvard Academy accused by 18 women of sexual harassment. Resigned.

Doute, Kristen. Doute and a fellow cast mate on *Vanderpump Rules*, called the police and falsely accused a Black cast mate of robbery. Doute was fired from the series.

Dreger, Alice. The former Professor of Bioethics and Medical History at Northwestern University wrote "Galileo's Middle Finger." According to Dreger's website, she was "denounced by Rush Limbaugh and the Lambda Literary Foundation." She resigned after being censored by the dean who also "instituted a censorship committee" for the faculty journal.

Easterbrook, Stephen. The CEO of McDonalds admitted to a consensual relationship with an employee, violating company policy. Fired.

Eller, Claudia. The Editor-in-Chief of *Variety* magazine wrote an opinion piece, taking responsibility for not doing enough to promote diversity in the industry. According to the *Los Angeles Times*, this led to a twitter spat with a reporter from another outlet. Sinha-Roy called out Eller for a discussion the two had years before on that very topic. Eller responded to the tweet, "When someone cops to something why would you try to criticize them? You sound really bitter." This upset others at *Variety* and a decision was made to place Eller on a two-month leave.

Fairstein, Linda. After Netflix aired a documentary falsely outlining Fairstein's involvement in the Central Park Five case, the chief prosecutor was subsequently canceled. She was forced to resign as a trustee of Vassar College and numerous awards & appearances were rescinded.

Fansler, Zach. Alaska State Representative accused of slapping a woman when she denied his sexual advances. Resigned.

Fahrenthold, Blake. U.S. Representative for Texas accused of sexual harassment and using taxpayer money to settle the claim. Resigned and dropped his re-election bid.

Fein, Bruce. According to wghb.org, the governing board of Harvard Law School's free speech organization withdrew its invitation to Fein (an alumnus and attorney). The topic concerned the rule of law in the age of Trump. Before the event, Fein was asked: "What are your views, as to the historical accuracy of the claim that an Armenian genocide occurred after the First World War?" Fein explained his thoughts on "the nature, nuances and historical basis." He believed the attack against the Armenians, "while ghastly, does not rise to the legal definition of 'genocide.'" Shortly thereafter, Fein received an email containing the following: "I regret to inform you that the Board of the Harvard Law School Forum must retract its invitation to speak at the Forum this spring. Unfortunately, the rest of the Board is not comfortable with inviting you to speak this spring as it appears our views on the Ottoman action against Armenians after World War I diverge slightly from yours."

Fells, Kendall. Organizing Director of the Service Employees International Union's Fight for 15 Campaign accused of harassment and employee misconduct. Resigned.

Ferro Jr., Michael. Chairman of Tronc accused of sexual advances. Resigned.

Fish, Hamilton. Publisher and President of *The New Republic* accused of inappropriate conduct. Resigned.

Franken, Al. U.S. Senator of Minnesota accused of groping & improper advances (multiple women). Resigned.

Franklin, Jeff. Showrunner for *Fuller House* accused of making verbally abusive/sexually charged comments on set. Removed.

Gastañaga, Claire Guthrie. According to thefire.org, the Executive Director of the ACLU was invited to guest-speak at College of William and Mary in October of 2017. Gastañaga was "shouted down" by Black Lives Matter protesters who were upset the ACLU supported the law suit of white nationalists involved in the Unite the Right rally in Charlottesville by chanting "ACLU, you protect Hitler too," and "ACLU, free speech for who?" Within 30 minutes, the event was cancelled. According to the school newspaper, *The Flat Hat*, students gathered around Gastañaga hoping to continue the conversation. The protestors then gathered around the group, chanting even louder, causing the students to disband. Taylor Reveley, the president of William and Mary, prepared a written statement in response to the protestors. He wrote, "Silencing certain voices in order to advance the cause of others is not acceptable in our community." He continued, "This stifles debate and prevents those who've come to hear a speaker, our students in particular, from asking questions, often hard questions, and from engaging in debate where the strength of ideas, not the power of shouting, is the currency."

Gillis, Shane. Comedian and new cast member of *Saturday Night Live*. Gillis and another comedian have a podcast called "Matt and Shane's Secret Podcast." According to *CNN*, *Saturday Night Live* hired Gillis as a new cast member, then found out he made "defamatory comments about Chinese Americans, LGBTQ people and women" during a podcast. Fired from *Saturday Night Live*.

Goddard, Gary. Founder of the Goddard Group accused of molesting eight former child actors. Stepped down.

Goodman, Wes. According to *The New York Times*, the Ohio State Representative admitted to "inappropriate behavior" and was accused of unwanted sexual advances towards other men. Resigned.

Greitens, Eric. According to *The New York Times*, the Missouri Governor was accused "of taking an explicit photo of a woman without her consent and threatening to blackmail her." Resigned.

Gunn, James. Disney fired the director of "Guardians of the Galaxy" after insensitive tweets resurfaced about AIDS victims, pedophilia and sexual assault. Shortly after his firing, colleagues, friends, family members and fans defended him by tweeting "RehireJamesGunn." The Washington Post reported a petition to rehire Gunn collected over 200,000 signatures and Gunn was ultimately rehired.

Haggis, Paul. The screenwriter, director, and founder of the charity, Artists for Peace & Justice was accused of rape and sexual assault. This led to his resignation form the charity.

Halperin, Mark. Political Journalist accused of sexual harassment by former co-workers. Several news networks severed ties with the journalist.

Hart, Kevin. The comedian posted homophobic tweets that recently resurfaced and Hart was pulled from hosting the Oscars.

Hazen, Don. Executive Editor, AlterNet accused of sexual harassment (multiple women). Resigned.

Herzog, Katie. The freelance journalist in Seattle published an article in *The Stranger* about trans people who "halt or reverse transitions." According to *The New York Times*, residents burned stacks of the magazine. She was also called a transphobe and did not feel welcome in lesbian bars. As a result, Herzog moved out of her hometown.

Hite, Cliff. Ohio Senator accused of sexual harassment (one known person). Fired.

Hoey, Clyde. Western Carolina University recently changed its auditorium name from Clyde Hoey to University Auditorium. Hoey a former N. Carolina governor opposed racial integration.

Hoover, Jeff. The Kentucky State Representative and House Speaker was accused of sexual harassment ultimately leading to his resignation.

Homan, Thomas. Former Director of the United States Immigration and Customs Enforcement Agency was scheduled to speak at UPenn. Protesters in support of abolishing ICE chanted so loudly before Homan's appearance, that the event was canceled five minutes after the scheduled start time.

Hybels, Bill. Lead Pastor of Willow Creek Church accused by former pastors/staff members of sexual misconduct. Retired.

Isaly, Sam. Managing Partner of Orbimed Advisors accused by multiple employees of sexual harassment & watching pornography in the workplace. Retired.

Irvin, Amy. The Executive Director of the American Abortion Fund was scheduled to speak at Loyola. Administrators compelled the

College Democrats to cancel the pro-choice speaker. The school was not funding the event but stated: "Irvin was too extreme and could potentially reflect badly on Loyola if outsiders were to believe Loyola had funded the event." Irvin's appearance was canceled even though the Loyola student code of conduct states: "Sponsorship of speakers does not imply approval or endorsement of the views expressed, either by the sponsoring group or by Loyola."

Iuzzini, Johnny. Chef/Judge on *The Great American Baking Show* accused of sexual harassment (multiple former employees). Fired.

Jacoby, William G. Editor of the *American Journal of Political Science* accused of sexual harassment from a former student. Resigned.

Jennings, Caleb. According to *The New York Times*, the Chicago organizer for Service Employees International Union was accused of "sexual misconduct and abusive behavior." Jennings was "found not guilty of assault in court." Fired.

Jolson, Al. Known as "The King of Blackface." The Fraternal Order of Police involved in a fundraiser for police officers, accused Jolson of being an "iconic racist figure." According to the *Baltimore Sun*, Jolson has been described as, "Far from being a racist, he befriended black entertainers and promoted their careers. No one considered him a racist."

Jordan, David Starr. Indian University approved a name change for Jordan Hall. David Starr Jordan, a former zoology professor and university president, supported eugenics.

Kaepernick, Colin. According to *USA Today*, Kaepernick, a pro football player and quarterback for the San Francisco 49's, chose to kneel during the national anthem in protest of "police brutality against people of color and systemic oppression." As a result of

Kaepernick's decision, owners of the NFL collectively denied him employment.

Kelly, R. The R & B Singer was accused of sexual assault and abuse by several young women (some underage). A #MuteRKelly tweet resulted in canceled concerts, dropped airplay, removal from Spotify's playlists (as a result of its new hateful conduct policy). Collaborators, such as Lady Gaga, Chance the Rapper and Celine Dion also requested the removal of their songs from streaming sites.

Kerrey, Bob. According to *Omaha World Herald*, the former Governor of Nebraska & United States Senator was scheduled as the commencement speaker at Creighton University. Ryan Hamilton, the Nebraska GOP executive director, requested Creighton to rescind Kerrey's invitation to speak at its ceremony because of Kerrey's pro-choice beliefs. In a press release, Hamilton stated: "Creighton is a Jesuit institution formally affiliated with the Catholic Church, one of the country's most consistent and reliable advocates for pro-life causes. Nebraska is a pro-life state and Republicans are a pro-life party. We strongly urge Creighton to take a stand for their pro-life values and find a more appropriate figure to honor at their upcoming commencement." Kerrey withdrew his acceptance believing he would cause a distraction.

Klobuchar, Amy. The Minnesota Senator was accused of failing to file charges against policemen involved in multiple shootings of African-Americans when she was a prosecutor. Klobuchar ultimately removed herself from consideration as Joe Biden's Vice Presidential nominee.

Krasner, Larry. The Philadelphia District Attorney was scheduled as a keynote speaker at Yale Law School. Student organizers rescinded their invitation to Krasner when he filed an appeal after Mumia Abu-Jamal, who was convicted of killing a police officer, received a favorable ruling.

Kreisberg, Andrew. Executive Producer of *Arrow*, *Supergirl*, and *The Flash* accused of sexual harassment and inappropriate physical contact. Fired.

Kruse, Jeff. Oregon State Senator accused of sexual harassment and inappropriate physical contact (multiple women). Resigned.

Lauer, Matt. According to *The New York Times*, the television news anchor was accused of "inappropriate sexual behavior toward a fellow staffer." Others accused Lauer of unwanted advances. Fired from NBC.

Lebsock, Steve. Colorado State Representative accused of sexual harassment (multiple women). Expelled by the Colorado House of Representatives.

Legutko, Ryszard. The scholar and far-right member of the European Parliament was scheduled to speak at Middlebury College. According to thefire.org, it was discovered Legutko made homophobic comments in the past, such as, "I don't understand why anyone should want to be proud of being a homosexual, be proud of what you do, not of being a homosexual." Citing security risks - the lecture was canceled. Soon thereafter, a political science student asked one of his professors if he would invite Legutko as a guest speaker in his classroom. The Professor agreed only if the student received unanimous support from the class-which he did. Ultimately, Legutko was able to speak protest-free and a peaceful protest was planned via Facebook.

Levine, James. According to *The New York Times*, an investigation into the conductor at the Metropolitan Opera "uncovered credible evidence" that Levine "engaged in sexually abusive and harassing conduct." Fired - he is suing for breach of contract and defamation.

Live PD. The TV series allowed viewers live access to "the country's busiest police forces." According to CNN, " A&E made the decision to cancel the show, citing "a critical time in our nation's history.

Loeffler, Kelly. According to ESPN, The United States Senator & co-owner of the WNBA team the Atlanta Dream, came under fire after making comments about the Black Lives Matter political organization. Loeffler claims to support the statement, "Black Lives Matter" but not the organization which she claims, "advocates things like defunding and abolishing the police, abolishing our military, emptying our prisons, destroying the nuclear family. It promotes violence and anti-Semitism. To me, this is not what our league stands for." Members of the WNBA league tried to force Loeffler to sell her ownership stake in the team, but have been unsuccessful.

Loftus, Dr. Elizabeth. The professor at the University of California Irvine was scheduled as a guest speaker at New York University. Preparations for her visit were being made when an article was published, mentioning her involvement in the Harvey Weinstein trial as an expert witness for the defense. Following the publication, Dr. Loftus received a letter from the university notifying her that they were canceling her speaking engagement for "circumstances beyond their control." Although it is uncertain whether their assertion was accurate, NYU has not responded to requests for an explanation regarding the cancelation.

Marciano, Paul. Executive Chairman of Guess, Inc. accused of sexual harassment & assault (multiple women). Replaced by his brother.

Martins, Peter. Ballet Master in Chief of the New York City Ballet accused of sexual harassment (multiple dancers). An internal investigation did not substantiate the claims. Retired.

McAleenan, Kevin. The Former Acting United States Secretary of Homeland Security was scheduled as the keynote speaker at a Georgetown University event. According to thefire.org, McAleenan was prevented from addressing the crowd when protesters "shouted him down" over his views on immigration. It was reported that McAleenan walked off the stage.

Meier, Richard. The acclaimed architect accused of exposing himself and/or touching several former employees. Resigned.

Mendoza, Antonio. California State Senator accused of improper advances (multiple women). Resigned.

Miller, T.J. The actor was accused of sexual assault and hitting a woman in college. Dropped as a Mucinex spokesperson and Comedy Central canceled a show Miller was working on.

Moonves, Leslie. President, Chairman & Chief Executive of CBS Corporation accused of sexual misconduct & retaliation against those who rejected his sexual advances. Resigned.

Moore, John. Mississippi State Representative accused of sexual harassment (multiple women) Resigned, citing health concerns.

Moore, Rob. Managing Editor of *The New York Daily News* accused of sexual harassment. Fired.

Najera, Rick. Director of CBS's *Diversity Showcase* accused of inappropriate and lewd comments. Resigned.

Napear, Grant. Former Sports Announcer for the Sacramento Kings Tweeted "ALL LIVES MATTER" and was subsequently fired.

Neal-Boylan, Leslie. Former Dean of Nursing at UMASS Lowell —following the George Floyd protests, Neal-Boylan addressed the current challenges and wrote, "Everyone's Life Matter." Subsequently fired.

Oreskes, Michael. Head of News at *NPR* and former *New York Times* editor accused of sexual harassment. Resigned.

Pacelle, Wayne. Chief Executive of the Humane Society accused of sexual harassment (forcible kissing & unwanted advances by three women). Resigned.

Parneros, Demos. Chief Executive of Barnes & Noble accused of sexual harassment by an executive assistant. Fired.

Palomarez, Javier. Chief Executive of the U.S. Hispanic Chamber of Commerce accused of financial impropriety and sexual assault (former staffer). Stepped down.

Pike, Albert. A statue of the former United States Senator who had a reputation of attacking civil rights advocates, was toppled by protesters in Washington, D.C.

Pinker, Steven. The Harvard Linguistics Professor & "distinguished fellow" at the Linguistic Society of America was a recent target of cancel culture. According to *The Federalist,* A letter was sent to the Linguistic Society of America by a group of linguistics professors requesting the removal of Dr. Pinker. It claimed: "Dr. Pinker has a history of speaking over genuine grievances and downplaying injustices, frequently by misrepresenting facts, and at the exact moments when Black and Brown people are mobilizing against systemic racism and for crucial changes."

Price, Roy. Head of Amazon Studios accused of making unwanted sexual advances. Resigned.

Rapoport, Adam. A picture of the former Editor-in-Chief at *Bon Appetit,* in brownface taken in 2004 and published in 2013, caused many former and current employees to speak out about their own experiences of discrimination. Rapoport resigned.

Reed, Adolph. The Black Marxist Scholar was invited to speak at the Democratic Socialist of America's New York Chapter. Reed was subsequently accused of downplaying racism and was canceled as a guest speaker.

Richards, Michael. The former *Seinfeld* actor appeared at a comedy club and verbally attacked Black hecklers. The rant was caught on tape and his TV spin-off, *The Michael Richards Show*, was canceled.

Roosevelt, Theodore. According to the *New York Times*, the decision to remove the bronze statue in front of the American Museum of Natural History in New York was made "because it explicitly depicts Black and Indigenous people as subjugated and racially inferior."

Rose, Charlie. Television Host accused of crude sexual advances (multiple women). Fired by CBS and PBS.

Rosenberg, Sid. The sports radio personality was scheduled at Seton Hall for a campus speech/debate. Rosenberg was disinvited to speak at the Town Hall event following a social media campaign led by students as a result of past disparaging remarks on race, women and sexual preferences.

Rosenthal, Paul. Colorado State Representative accused of groping. Various complaints were dismissed by the Colorado General Assembly. Rosenthal lost his re-election bid.

Sauer, Nick. Illinois State Representative accused by a former girlfriend, of releasing nude photos of her on Instagram. Resigned.

Savino, Chris. Creator of Nickelodeon's *The Loud House*, accused of sexual harassment (multiple people). Fired.

Scoble, Robert. Co-founder of the Transformation Group accused of sexual assault (multiple women). Resigned.

Schneiderman, Eric. Attorney General of New York accused of assaulting four women. Resigned.

Schroeder, Stassi Schroeder and a fellow cast mate on Vanderpump Rules, called the police and falsely accused a Black cast mate of robbery. Ultimately, Schroeder was fired from Vanderpump Rules, dropped from United Talent Agency and Metro Public Relations, and lost several sponsorships.

Shapiro, Ben. As a former editor at *Breitbart*, the Editor-in-Chief of the *Dailey Wire*, author, and conservative political commentator, Ben Shapiro has been invited and disinvited to numerous college campuses across the nation. Thefire.org, has cited Shapiro in its "Disinvitation Database" eight times since 2016. Out of the eight, four of them resulted in a revocation of the invite with the latest occurring in 2018.

Shapiro, Paul. Vice President of the Humane Society accused of sexual harassment (multiple women). Resigned.

Schoen, Dan. Minnesota Senator accused of sexual harassment (multiple women). Resigned.

Shooter, Don. An investigation into the Arizona State Representative found he sexually harassed several women. Expelled by the Arizona House of Representatives.

Silverman, Sarah. The comedian and actress engaged in a blackface skit on "*The Sarah Silverman Project*" several years ago but recently resurfaced. The night before she was scheduled to begin filming a new movie, she was told her role had been replaced.

Silverstein, Ira. Illinois Senator accused of sexual harassment. Resigned as caucus chair and lost his re-election bid.

Singer, Bryan. Director and Producer accused of sexually assaulting a 17 year-old male. Fired from *Bohemian Rhapsody* as director (but retains a director's credit) and lost his executive producer credit for the television show, *Legion.*

Smith, Kate. After recording two songs deemed appropriate at the time but considered racially insensitive today, Smith is being canceled posthumously. The New York Yankees stopped playing her rendition of "God Bless America" and the Philadelphia Flyers removed her statue from its stadium.

Smollet, Jussie. According to CNN, the actor on the TV show *Empire*, accused two men of an attack by pouring an unknown substance on him while "yelling out racial and homophobic slurs." Smollet's character was cut from the final two episodes.

Souki, Joseph M. Hawaii State Representative accused of unwanted sexual advances (multiple women). Resigned.

Spacey, Kevin. Accused of forcing himself on a minor, leading more men to come forward with sexual misconduct allegations. Spacey was dropped from *House of Cards* and replaced in *All the Money in the World.*

Steele, Lockhart. The Editorial Director of Vox Media was accused of sexual harassment (one known person). Fired.

Stein, Lorin. Editor of the *Paris Review* accused of unspecified conduct with multiple female employees/writers. Resigned.

Stewart, Jannique. Pro-Life Speaker with the Life Training Institute who openly supports traditional marriage between a man and woman was cancelled as a guest speaker at Cornell University once she made it clear she would be sharing her beliefs.

Summers, Lawrence. Former President of Harvard was forced to resign following his comment on why women have not achieved the same level of success in STEM as men.

Sweeney, David. Chief News Editor at NPR accused of sexual harassment (multiple women). Resigned.

Templer, Karl. Stylist & Creative Director of *Interview Magazine* accused of unwanted touching of breasts/crotches by three women. Resigned.

Tooke, Tony. Chief of the United States Forest Service accused of sexual misconduct. Resigned.

Uzan, Bernard. Co-director of Florida Grand Opera's Young Artists program accused of sexual misconduct by four female singers. Resigned.

Weinberger, Eric. According to *The New York Times*, the president of the Bill Simmons Media Group accused of sending "lewd messages" to a former NFL Network stylist. A suit was filed and later settled. Weinberger was initially suspended but later left the company.

Weinstein, Harvey. Producer & co-Founder of the Weinstein Company accused of sexual assault by multiple women was fired & convicted of rape and sexual assault. His case is on appeal (I have consulted with his lawyers).

Westlake, Dean. Alaska State Representative accused of sexual harassment and groping (multiple aides). Resigned.

Westwick, Ed. Actor in *Ordeal by Innocence* accused of sexual assault (multiple women). Replaced by another actor (prosecutors did not press charges citing lack of evidence).

Wieseltier, Leon. According to *The Atlantic*, in 2017, Wieseltier was accused of sexual harassment along with approximately 60 other men in the publishing industry. An anonymous document titled, "SHITTY MEDIA MEN" circulated among members of the media and according to the spreadsheet, Wieseltier was listed as "workplace harassment." As a result, the financial backer for Wieseltier's new culture magazine ended its relationship with the "legendary" literary editor.

Wilson, Woodrow. Princeton University removed Woodrow Wilson's name from its School of Public Affairs and one of its residential colleges. According to insidehighered.com, Princeton initially considered the removal in 2016 as a result of Wilson's "segregationist policies." In light of the recent killings of several Black citizens, they changed the name. Monmouth University also removed Wilson's name from its marquee building. And in Camden, N.J., his name was removed from a school. According to *The New York Times*, Camden's Superintendent, Latrina McCombs stated, "Our students will walk into a new building not tied to a building with a racist legacy." Wilson was awarded the Nobel Peace Prize in 1920 for his efforts in ending Word War I and for establishing the League of Nations.

Wynn, Steve. Chief Executive, Wynn Resorts denied accusations of harassing female employees. Resigned.

Appendix II: A Letter on Justice and Open Debate, from *Harper's Magazine*, July 7th, 2020[1]

Our cultural institutions are facing a moment of trial. Powerful protests for racial and social justice are leading to overdue demands for police reform, along with wider calls for greater equality and inclusion across our society, not least in higher education, journalism, philanthropy, and the arts. But this needed reckoning has also intensified a new set of moral attitudes and political commitments that tend to weaken our norms of open debate and toleration of differences in favor of ideological conformity. As we applaud the first development, we also raise our voices against the second. The forces of illiberalism are gaining strength throughout the world and have a powerful ally in Donald Trump, who represents a real threat to democracy. But resistance must not be allowed to harden into its own brand of dogma or coercion—which right-wing demagogues are already exploiting. The democratic inclusion we want can be achieved only if we speak out against the intolerant climate that has set in on all sides.

The free exchange of information and ideas, the lifeblood of a liberal society, is daily becoming more constricted. While we have

---

1   Available online at: https://harpers.org/a-letter-on-justice-and-open-debate/

come to expect this on the radical right, censoriousness is also spreading more widely in our culture: an intolerance of opposing views, a vogue for public shaming and ostracism, and the tendency to dissolve complex policy issues in a blinding moral certainty. We uphold the value of robust and even caustic counter-speech from all quarters. But it is now all too common to hear calls for swift and severe retribution in response to perceived transgressions of speech and thought. More troubling still, institutional leaders, in a spirit of panicked damage control, are delivering hasty and disproportionate punishments instead of considered reforms. Editors are fired for running controversial pieces; books are withdrawn for alleged inauthenticity; journalists are barred from writing on certain topics; professors are investigated for quoting works of literature in class; a researcher is fired for circulating a peer-reviewed academic study; and the heads of organizations are ousted for what are sometimes just clumsy mistakes. Whatever the arguments around each particular incident, the result has been to steadily narrow the boundaries of what can be said without the threat of reprisal. We are already paying the price in greater risk aversion among writers, artists, and journalists who fear for their livelihoods if they depart from the consensus, or even lack sufficient zeal in agreement.

This stifling atmosphere will ultimately harm the most vital causes of our time. The restriction of debate, whether by a repressive government or an intolerant society, invariably hurts those who lack power and makes everyone less capable of democratic participation. The way to defeat bad ideas is by exposure, argument, and persuasion, not by trying to silence or wish them away. We refuse any false choice between justice and freedom, which cannot exist without each other. As writers we need a culture that leaves us room for experimentation, risk taking, and even mistakes. We need to preserve the possibility of good-faith disagreement without dire professional consequences. If we won't defend the very thing on which our work depends, we shouldn't expect the public or the state to defend it for us.

Anne Applebaum

Marie Arana, author

Margaret Atwood

John Banville

Mia Bay, historian

Louis Begley, writer

Roger Berkowitz, Bard College

Paul Berman, writer

Sheri Berman, Barnard College

Reginald Dwayne Betts, poet

Neil Blair, agent

David W. Blight, Yale University

Jennifer Finney Boylan, author

David Bromwich

David Brooks, columnist

Ian Buruma, Bard College

Lea Carpenter

Noam Chomsky, MIT (emeritus)

Nicholas A. Christakis, Yale University

Roger Cohen, writer

Ambassador Frances D. Cook, ret.

Drucilla Cornell, Founder, uBuntu Project

Kamel Daoud

Meghan Daum, writer

Gerald Early, Washington University-St. Louis

Jeffrey Eugenides, writer

Dexter Filkins

Federico Finchelstein, The New School

Caitlin Flanagan

Richard T. Ford, Stanford Law School

Kmele Foster

David Frum, journalist

Francis Fukuyama, Stanford University

Atul Gawande, Harvard University

Todd Gitlin, Columbia University

Kim Ghattas

Malcolm Gladwell

Michelle Goldberg, columnist

Rebecca Goldstein, writer

Anthony Grafton, Princeton University

David Greenberg, Rutgers University

Linda Greenhouse

Rinne B. Groff, playwright

Sarah Haider, activist

Jonathan Haidt, NYU-Stern

Roya Hakakian, writer

Shadi Hamid, Brookings Institution

Jeet Heer, The Nation

Katie Herzog, podcast host

Susannah Heschel, Dartmouth College

Adam Hochschild, author

Arlie Russell Hochschild, author

Eva Hoffman, writer

Coleman Hughes, writer/ Manhattan Institute

Hussein Ibish, Arab Gulf States Institute

Michael Ignatieff

Zaid Jilani, journalist

Bill T. Jones, New York Live Arts

Wendy Kaminer, writer

Matthew Karp, Princeton University

Garry Kasparov, Renew Democracy Initiative

Daniel Kehlmann, writer

Randall Kennedy

Khaled Khalifa, writer

Parag Khanna, author

Laura Kipnis, Northwestern University

Frances Kissling, Center for Health, Ethics, Social Policy

Enrique Krauze, historian

Anthony Kronman, Yale University

Joy Ladin, Yeshiva University

Nicholas Lemann, Columbia University

Mark Lilla, Columbia University

Susie Linfield, New York University

Damon Linker, writer

Dahlia Lithwick, Slate

Steven Lukes, New York University

John R. MacArthur, publisher, writer

Wynton Marsalis, Jazz at Lincoln Center

Kati Marton, author

Debra Mashek, scholar

Deirdre McCloskey, University of Illinois at Chicago

John McWhorter, Columbia University

Uday Mehta, City University of New York

Andrew Moravcsik, Princeton University

Yascha Mounk, Persuasion

Samuel Moyn, Yale University

Meera Nanda, writer and teacher

Cary Nelson, University of Illinois at Urbana-Champaign

Olivia Nuzzi, New York Magazine

Mark Oppenheimer, Yale University

Dael Orlandersmith, writer/ performer

George Packer

Nell Irvin Painter, Princeton University (emerita)

Greg Pardlo, Rutgers University – Camden

Orlando Patterson, Harvard University

Steven Pinker, Harvard University

Letty Cottin Pogrebin

Katha Pollitt, writer

Claire Bond Potter, The New School

Taufiq Rahim

Zia Haider Rahman, writer

Jennifer Ratner-Rosenhagen, University of Wisconsin

Jonathan Rauch, Brookings Institution/The Atlantic

Neil Roberts, political theorist

Melvin Rogers, Brown University

Kat Rosenfield, writer

Loretta J. Ross, Smith College

J.K. Rowling

Salman Rushdie, New York University

Karim Sadjadpour, Carnegie Endowment

Daryl Michael Scott, Howard University

Diana Senechal, teacher and writer

Jennifer Senior, columnist

Judith Shulevitz, writer

Jesse Singal, journalist

Anne-Marie Slaughter

Andrew Solomon, writer

Deborah Solomon, critic and biographer

Allison Stanger, Middlebury College

Paul Starr, American Prospect/ Princeton University

Wendell Steavenson, writer

Gloria Steinem, writer and activist

Nadine Strossen, New York Law School

Ronald S. Sullivan Jr., Harvard Law School

Kian Tajbakhsh, Columbia University

Zephyr Teachout, Fordham University

Cynthia Tucker, University of South Alabama

Adaner Usmani, Harvard University

Chloe Valdary

Helen Vendler, Harvard University

Judy B. Walzer

Michael Walzer

Eric K. Washington, historian

Caroline Weber, historian

Randi Weingarten, American Federation of Teachers

Bari Weiss

Cornel West

Sean Wilentz, Princeton University

Garry Wills

Thomas Chatterton Williams, writer

Robert F. Worth, journalist and author

Molly Worthen, University of North Carolina at Chapel Hill

Matthew Yglesias

Emily Yoffe, journalist

Cathy Young, journalist

Fareed Zakaria

Institutions are listed for identification purposes only.

Appendix III: What Has Been Cancelled: A Brief Résumé of My Life and Achievements[2]

Professor Alan M. Dershowitz is a Brooklyn native who has been called one of the nation's "most distinguished defenders of individual rights," an "international treasure," "the best-known criminal lawyer in the world," and "the top lawyer of last resort." He has been named "the Jewish state's lead attorney in the court of public opinion," "the nation's most peripatetic civil liberties lawyer" and America's most "public Jewish Defender." He is the Felix Frankfurter Professor of Law, Emeritus, at Harvard Law School. Dershowitz, a graduate of Brooklyn College and Yale Law School, joined the Harvard Law School faculty at age twenty-five, becoming a full professor at twenty-eight—the youngest in the school's history—and became an Emeritus professor after fifty years of teaching and 10,000 students. At eighty-one, he was the oldest lawyer ever to argue before the Senate in a presidential impeachment case, having made the constitutional arguments against removing President Trump.

Dershowitz has been called "one of the sharpest legal minds of all time," "a masterful advocate," and the "winningest" criminal

---

2   For a more complete account, see Dershowitz, *Taking the Stand: My Life in the Law*

appellate lawyer in modern history, and has argued hundreds of appeals in courts throughout the nation and around the world. He was involved in many of the most significant legal cases and constitutional cases of the past half century, including the Pentagon Papers case, the impeachments of Presidents Clinton and Trump, *Bush v. Gore*, and the cases of Julian Assange, O.J. Simpson, Natan Sharansky, Nelson Mandela, Mike Tyson, Patricia Hearst, Michael Milken, Jeffrey Epstein, Mark Rich, and Leona Helmsley. He has won the vast majority of his homicide and capital cases (approximately twenty-three out of twenty-seven) and has never lost a client to the death penalty. He continues to consult actively on both transnational and domestic criminal and civil liberty cases. He devotes half of his practice to pro bono cases and causes.

Dershowitz has also published more than 1,000 articles in magazines, newspapers, journals, and blogs. These include *The New York Times*, for which he has written numerous op-eds, book reviews, and articles for the News of the Week in Review, as well as for the magazine and entertainment sections. He has also written for the *Wall Street Journal*, the *Washington Post*, the *Boston Globe*, the *Los Angeles Times*, the *Daily News*, the *Boston Herald*, the *Harvard Law Review*, the *Yale Law Journal*, the *Huffington Post*, *Gatestone*, *Newsmax*, the *Jerusalem Post*, *Ha'aretz*, and *Algemeiner*, as well as for publications in Germany, South Africa, Australia, Israel, Canada, Italy, and other countries. Professor Dershowitz is the author of more than forty non-fiction works and three novels with a worldwide audience, including the *New York Times* number-one bestseller *Chutzpah* and six other national bestsellers. His autobiography, *Taking the Stand: My Life in the Law*, was published in 2013. *Defending Israel: The Story of My Relationship with my Most Challenging Client* was published in 2019. His recent books are *The Case Against Impeaching Trump*, 2019; *Guilt by Accusation: The Challenge of Proving Innocence in the Age of #MeToo*, 2019; *The Case for Liberalism in an Age of Extremism: or, Why I Left the Left But Can't Join the Right*, published in 2020; *Defending the Constitution*, published in 2020; and *Cancel Culture*, published in 2020.

His writing has been praised by Truman Capote, Saul Bellow,

William Styron, David Mamet, Aharon Appelfeld, A.B. Yehoshua, Elie Wiesel, Richard North Patterson, Steven Pinker, and Henry Louis Gates, Jr. More than a million of his books—translated in many languages—have been sold worldwide.

In addition to his numerous law review articles and books about criminal and constitutional law, he has written, taught, and lectured about history, philosophy, psychology, literature, mathematics, theology, music, sports—and even delicatessens (he was commissioned by *The New York Times* to write an op-ed comparing all of New York's delis and selecting the best pastrami; he picked Katz's).

He has been the recipient of numerous honorary doctor degrees and academic awards, including a Guggenheim Fellowship for his work on human rights, a fellowship at The Center for the Advanced Study of Behavioral Sciences, and several Dean's Awards for his books.

Dershowitz has lectured in venues throughout the world, including The Kremlin, The Knesset, The French National Assembly, The House of Lords, the Sydney Opera House, Carnegie Hall, Lincoln Center, Boston Garden, and Madison Square Garden, as well as at many of the world's great universities.

In 1983, the Anti-Defamation League of the B'nai B'rith presented him with the William O. Douglas First Amendment Award for his "compassionate eloquent leadership and persistent advocacy in the struggle for civil and human rights." In presenting the award, Nobel Laureate Elie Wiesel said: "If there had been a few people like Alan Dershowitz during the 1930s and 1940s, the history of European Jewry might have been different."

He has been the subject of two *New Yorker* cartoons, a *New York Times* crossword puzzle, and a Trivial Pursuit question. A Sandwich at Fenway Park has been named after him—pastrami, of course.

He is married to Carolyn Cohen, a Ph.D. psychologist. He has three children, one a film producer, one a lawyer for the Women's National Basketball Association, and one a professional actor. He also has two grandchildren, both studying to become doctors.

Dershowitz, a longtime Democrat, has always put the Constitution above partisanship and principle above popularity.

Acknowledgments

I could not have written this book without the help of Maura Kelley, Aaron Voloj, Tonya Letterman, Oren Eades, and Tony Lyons. I could not write any of my books without the support and love of my family and friends, especially my wife, Carolyn, my children, and my grandchildren. Thanks also to Alan Rothfeld, Alan Zwiebel, and others who offered suggestions and critiques.